The Case for Germany.

The Case for Germany.

A Study of Modern Germany.

Arthur Pillans Laurie

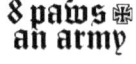

The Scriptorium

First published in 1939: *The Case for Germany: A study of Modern Germany,* Internationaler Verlag, Berlin W15., 1939.

Reprint: Copyright ©2003, 2022 by The Scriptorium
wintersonnenwende.com
versandbuchhandelscriptorium.com

Our cover design shows a scene from the Reichsparteitag 1937: the great assembly of political leaders on the searchlight-illuminated Zeppelin Field in Nuremberg, September 10, 1937.

Print edition ISBN 978-1-7775436-4-8
ebook ISBN 978-1-7775436-5-5

First Printing, 2003
Second Printing, 2022

All rights reserved. No part of this book may be reproduced in any manner whatsoever without written permission except in the case of brief quotations embodied in critical articles and reviews.

CONTENTS

Some Words in Advance 1

1 Der Führer 4

2 The Beleaguered City 15

3 National Socialism 19

4 The Nazi Rallys at Nuremberg 29

5 The Foreign Policy of Germany 36

6 England and Germany 45

7 March 7th 1936, a Most Important Date 51

8 The Real Enemy of Europe 56

9 Communism versus National Socialism 60

10 The Union of the German People of Austria and the Sudeten Germans With the German People of the Reich 66

11 Acts of "Aggression" by Germany 79

|v|

CONTENTS

12 | The Dance of Death 85

13 | Our Future Policy Towards Germany 93

14 | The Hitler Youth Movement 100

15 | The Winter Help Organization 104

16 | National Socialism and the Protestant Church 110

17 | Economics 120

18 | The Four Years' Plan 142

19 | The German Colonies 145

20 | The Labour Front 150

21 | Agriculture 160

22 | Munich and After 173

23 | Appendix 189

Some Words in Advance

Dedication
It is with admiration and gratitude for the great work he has done for the German people that I dedicate this book to the Führer.

A. P. L

To the Reader
There are two sides to every question. You have read one side in our Press for six years. This book gives the other side.

A. P. L.

Preface
It is a great pleasure to me to introduce the public to Dr. Laurie's valuable book on modern Germany. He is best known to the world as a brilliant scientist, but he has found time in the intervals of his work to pursue with ardour the task upon which every sensible member of the British and German races should be engaged - namely the establishment of good relations and a better understanding between these two great nations.

Dr. Laurie knows full well that this friendship is the keystone to peace in Europe - nay, in the whole world.

He is one of the small group who founded the Association known as "The Link", whose sole aim is to get Britons and Germans to know and understand one another better. He is one of the most zealous workers in this good cause in the country.

He writes of the National Socialist movement with knowledge and great sympathy.

The particular value of this book lies in the fact that it is written by a foreigner, who cannot be accused of patriotic excess in his interpretation of the great work done by Herr Hitler and his associates. I recommend this volume with confidence to all people who are genuinely impressed with the desire to understand one of the greatest - and most bloodless - revolutions in history.

BARRY DOMVILE
Robin's Tree
8th May 1939.

"As we advance in our social knowledge, we shall endeavour to make our governments paternal as well as judicial; that is, to establish such laws and authorities as may at once direct us in our occupations, protect us against our follies, and visit us in our distresses; a government which shall repress dishonesty, as now it punishes theft; which shall show how the discipline of the masses may be brought to aid the toils of peace, as the discipline of the masses has hitherto knit the sinews of battle; a government which shall have its soldiers of the ploughshare as well as its soldiers of the sword, and which shall distribute more proudly its golden crosses of industry - golden as the glow of the harvest - than it now grants its bronze crosses of honour - bronzed with the crimson of blood."

RUSKIN.
Political Economy of Art.

"All front fighters fought side by side and went through an inferno. They are all comparable to the heroes of the ancient world. It was the manhood of the nations in their prime who fought and experienced the horrors of modern war.

In another war the flower of the nations' men and women will have to fight. Europe will be destroyed if the best in all of the nations are wiped out. A new conflict will exceed even the ghastly tragedies of the Great War.

I believe that those who rattle the sabres have not participated in war. I know that war veterans speak and think differently.

They energetically desire to prevent another conflict. I hope that the men who are standing before me can contribute to preserve the peace of the world - a peace of honour and equality for all.

Let us not talk of prestige as between the victors and the defeated. This is my one request: Forget what has divided the nations before and remember that history has advanced."

Field Marshal GOERING
addressing the British and German war veterans.

1

Der Führer

*"De l'audace et encore de
l'audace et toujours de l'audace."*

It has often been said here of the Führer that he was "only a house painter" or that he had "no education", and the general tendency of opinion in England is that he was not a public school man and therefore is not much good. This attitude shows not only a regrettable snobbishness, but a total ignorance of the origin of so many great men. It is an error which we in Scotland are not likely to fall into, as so many of our famous Scotsmen have come from a similar stock, and have had a similar upbringing and education to that of the Führer.

The Highland crofter with his fierce independence, and the poor Scottish student who worked on the farm all summer to pay his university fees, are our equivalent to the finest type of European peasant, who produces a Mussolini, and a Hitler, and the small farmers of America who produced an Abraham Lincoln.

It is among the peasants of Europe that the old customs and traditions are maintained; the townspeople tend to become all of one pattern, and it is to the country that we must go to find the old costumes handed down for centuries, and the old legends and fairy tales. The people in the mountain and forest districts of Germany still live in the houses, and wear on gala days the costumes with which the Grimms fairy tales are illustrated; through these tales we live in an imaginary world in our childhood, with which the familiar Grimms fairy tales are illustrated; through these tales we live in an imaginary world in our childhood which is the familiar every day world to them. However strong may be our link with Germany in later life, through the Protestant religion which we owe to her, and through her philosophy and music, the ties formed at our most impressionable age are with the peasant.

In the district of Waldviertel, lives a race of peasants who, in spite of having been part of the Austrian Empire, still speak the Bavarian dialect, and have clung fiercely to their traditions and racial independance. In 1672 a son was born to two of these peasants who bore the name of Stephan Hitler. His descendants lived on in the same district, until Alois Hitler, the Führer's father, determined to see the world, and set off on foot for Vienna. He became a Customs official, but love of the soil was strong in him, and he soon bought a farm in the beautiful district where the Inn joins the Danube, where he established his family, and to which he went on his retirement to take up again the life of a farmer which had been led by his ancestors.

It was here that Hitler passed his early childhood, and attended the monastery school where he first saw the Swastika carved on the arch of a stone well.

As a boy his desire was to be an artist. On the death of his parents he went to Vienna with a few coins in his pocket taking his portfolio of drawings with which he hoped to gain entrance to the Vienna art school. "You will never be a painter", said the Professor who glanced through his drawings, "but you show some talent for architecture". An interesting prophesy for the future of the boy who was to superintend the rebuilding of Berlin.

Rejected as a pupil both at the school of art and architecture, he found himself alone in Vienna with only a few coins between him and starvation. Building was going on everywhere and he found employment as a builder's labourer: the boy of 18 entering on a life of desperate poverty learnt to know all that was most sordid and cruel in the life of a great city. For long his only home was the corner of a cellar which he shared with other workmen. His fellow workmen were all followers of Karl Marx, and endless discussions went on in which young Hitler joined. He became convinced that the Socialists and Communists were on the wrong lines, refused to join the trade union and for this refusal suffered an early martyrdom, - he had no sooner got a job than his fellow workmen had him dismissed.

During this period he learnt the close connection between the Socialist movement in Vienna and the Jews. He has told us of his astonishment when he met in the street a Rabbi with long locks dressed in his caftan. He realised for the first time the existence in the heart of his civilisation of a people of an Eastern race and Eastern religion, foreign to all his racial and religious traditions and exercising an enormous influence through their control of finance. A people bound together by devotion to their race, which had survived being scattered broadcast through the world and persecuted through the centuries.

Finding it impossible to earn his living as a labourer unless he accepted the teaching of Karl Marx, he managed to pick up a scanty living by painting and selling cards. Many of his sketches made at this time survive, and show considerable artistic talent. After a time he migrated from Vienna to Munich and found a lodging with a small working tailor's family. He continued to earn a small pittance by his painted cards, and began to devour all the books he could get out of the public library on history and politics. The tailor and his family have always remained his good friends, and have the pleasantest recollection of the courteous young Austrian who was adored by the children and made his good landlady anxious for his health by his omniverous reading on history and politics, which often continued through the night. He denied himself bread in order to have the means to visit the theatre, especially the great works of Wagner whom he revered and still reveres today.

When war broke out he got permission from Austria to join a German regiment, and went joyfully to fight for his beloved Fatherland;

THE CASE FOR GERMANY.

at last, he felt, he could do something for Germany. He was chosen for the dangerous task of dispatch carrier from the trenches, was twice decorated for valour, was wounded, and won the affection and admiration of his fellow soldiers. His final decoration, the Iron Cross of the First Class, was won for capturing single handed a small French force and leading them back to his own trenches by sheer bluff and personality. At the close of the war he was blinded by a gas attack and lost his sight for some time, and ultimately returned to Munich still in the army.

Munich like the rest of Germany was in a state of anarchy and after a desperate struggle had suppressed a Communist rising which committed the most brutal atrocities. Hitler was employed to lecture to the troops to correct the disaffection among them and show them the follies of Communism.

A few months after his return the disastrous terms of the Treaty of Versailles were made known to the Germans. They were received with a feeling of utter dismay which was soon succeeded by one of hopeless despair. Hitler in the meantime had discovered during his lectures to the soldiers where his real future lay, and determined to return to civilian life and devote himself to politics. He investigated all the various groups which had formed themselves, each sure that they had the means of saving Germany, but none of them had grasped what seemed to Hitler the only road to salvation. He alone conceived the bold idea of refusing to accept the exactions of the Treaty of Versailles; but how was he, an unknown soldier, to get his ideas to the people of Germany?

One night he read a pamphlet, which had been given him at a meeting, by a workman called Anton Drexler, and realised that here at last was someone who was thinking along the right lines. Next evening he went to a meeting of this *"Deutsche Arbeiterpartei"*, a group of seven men with only 7.50 marks for funds, which was later to emerge as the National Socialist Party and sweep the whole of Germany.

Hitler inevitably became their leader and convinced them that the only chance of success was to hold public meetings. One of their first modest ventures was a meeting in the Munich *Hofbräukeller*, which held about 130 people. Hitler rose to address them and laid before them his whole plan for regenerating Germany. As he spoke the audience became wildly enthusiastic. He realised that he had the gift of oratory, and that by the use of this gift he could rouse Germany to action. The audience went out to spread everywhere the name of Hitler. Their future meetings grew larger and funds began to flow into the empty cash box. The Socialists became alarmed and decided to break up Hitler's meetings by physical violence; but he had foreseen this development and had called to him a handful of his old comrades of the battlefield and organised them as a militant body whom he called his Storm Troopers.

In November 1921 he decided to hold a great mass demonstration to test the real strength of the new movement, and if it succeeded to spread his organisation over the whole Reich. The Socialists determined that it should fail, and arranged to make an attack at the meeting which would smash the movement once and for all. The audience sat at little tables and refreshed themselves with beer while listening to the speaker. In Munich these beer mugs are heavy earthenware vessels. While Hitler was speaking the Socialists had been storing the empty mugs under their tables for ammunition, and at a given signal began hurling them at the heads of the audience and at Hitler who was standing on a table. During the rain of mugs Hitler never moved, and by some miracle was not hit. His Storm Troopers went promptly into action and though they were unarmed and their opponents had knives and other ugly weapons and greatly outnumbered them, the Storm Troopers after a desperate fight drove them out of the meeting. The scene was one of the wildest description and the hall was littered with broken mugs and smashed tables and chairs. Hitler calmly continued his speech where he had left off as if nothing had happened. Henceforth the Storm Troopers were known as "Storm Detachment" (*Sturm Abteilung* or SA.). While the Nazi movement was spreading through Bavaria, the Bavarians were getting more and more dissatisfied with the central government in Berlin, and a movement was spreading to separate Bavaria from the Republic. The Bavarian Minister von Knilling appointed Herr von Kahr as Commissar with almost absolute power. Herr von Kahr broke off relations with Berlin and was joined in his revolt by the heads of the army and the police in Bavaria. There was talk of a march on Berlin, while Ebert was considering the possibility of ordering the army of the Republic to march on Bavaria. Von Kahr and Hitler were in agreement, but von Kahr hesitated and failed to push the rebellion. On November 9th 1923, Hitler and Ludendorff were marching through Munich at the head of their comrades and fellow members through cheering crowds, when they were stopped by a cordon of police who fired upon them. The scene was one of the wildest panic, the street was strewn with dead and wounded, eighteen of Hitler's comrades were killed, and Hitler was thrown down injuring his shoulder.

This attack by the police was followed up by the arrest of Hitler and many of his party.

At his trial he made a speech in which he unfolded his whole policy; a speech which made a great impression in Germany. "It is not you, Gentlemen", - he told the Court - "who pass judgment on us. We shall be judged before the eternal bar of history." He was condemned to five years imprisonment in the fortress of Landsberg, a sentence which was afterwards commuted to nine months, and was soon joined in prison by many of his followers who were allowed by the prison rules to mix together in the daytime. While there letters and presents poured in from all over Germany, but his organisation was rapidly falling to pieces without the presence of its leader. It was during his imprisonment that he dictated *Mein Kampf* to Hess.

When he left prison in December 1924 he had come to the conclusion that a revolution based on a *coup d'etat* did not provide a permanent foundation on which to build a new state, and determined to undertake the colossal task of converting the whole German people and obtaining power by their votes. In spite of being forbidden to speak in several of the German federal states, his movement made rapid progress, and returned larger and larger numbers of members to the Reichstag at each election.

The work of building up this great organisation was stupendous, and during elections he flew in a plane all over Germany speaking everywhere and organising his followers. Finally he had a large majority over any other party in the Reichstag, and Hindenburg conferred on him the post of Chancellor, on January 30, 1933. Hitler asked the Reichstag for absolute power for four years; this was granted, and afterwards confirmed by a plebiscite of the whole German people.

Placed in power, he did not follow the usual practice of Dictators and shoot his opponents. The more dangerous enemies of the new government were put in concentration camps, where they suffered no more hardships than the common soldier. Civil servants opposed to him, and Jewish professors and heads of institutions, were pensioned off at the full value they would have received in old age. Then began the vast task of re-organising Germany; **the most bloodless revolution the world has ever seen had been accomplished.**

One cannot read the story of Hitler's early life without realising that everything went to form his mind for his future task. Consciously his ambition was to become a painter, but his early absorption in history and geography pointed in another direction. As a young boy, he came to realise what it meant to be separated from Germany, and to live in an Empire which is largely dominated by alien Slavonic influences. He read a history of the war of 1870 when he was a boy, and asked himself, why did we not go to the help of the Germans? The answer was plain. Because although we are Germans, we are divided from our blood brothers; the peoples would have joined, but the outside influence of rival dynasties kept them apart. Can we not see in this deep impression the reason behind his resolve to unite Austria and Germany, and his determination to bring the Sudeten Germans back to their fatherland?

He has denounced the folly of conquering and subduing foreign peoples. He had a perfect example before him in his youth, in the endless struggles to subdue the turbulent slav populations of the Austrian Empire, which finally caused its destruction. He was horrified when he visited as a young man the Austrian parliament, and found it full of Slavs who were making long speeches in languages which only a few could understand, and whose racial hatreds finally boiled up into a free fight.

The great social reforms which he has carried out can in the same way be attributed to his early experience. His sufferings of poverty, uncertainty of employment, and starvation in Vienna, when he was left an orphan at eighteen and had to become a labourer, made a deep impression on his mind, and unconsciously again, fate was shaping his destiny, giving him by this harsh treatment an understanding and insight into the difficulties and struggles of the working classes, which he could never have had otherwise. He has fought and conquered for Germany the terrible disease of unemployment, remembering his own misery when he was workless, and the pressing anxiety of where the next meal was to come from.

Brought into contact with Communism, the accepted faith of his fellow workmen, he was faced at an early age with fundamental political problems. Communism aims at a class war which would split Europe horizontally and result in an international communist state. Hitler saw in nationalism an emotional force which could unite all the peoples of a nation in a common purpose of justice for all classes. Communism appeals to hate, and denies the national bond, while nationalism appeals to the natural good feeling between the members of the same community. Communism is therefore necessarily anti-Christian, and nationalism is Christian, so long as it is used as a motive for internal reform, and does not result, as it has done so often in the past, in the proof of patriotism being the extent of our hatred of other nations. Brought into intimate contact with Communism as an active political force, and not as a subject for discussion in the study, he learnt to hate it, and to hate the men who were exploiting the workmen for their own purposes. His contact with Communism was therefore a part of his training for his future task; still a boy in years, he had to choose between the risk of starvation or the acceptance of Communism, and he chose to suffer hunger rather than bow the knee to the god of hate and class war.

As a soldier in the battlefield, he was to learn the horror and the mad futility of war, and the wickedness of hatred between nation and nation. **Patriotism, according to Hitler, means, thou shalt love the people of thine own nation as thyself. Patriotism according to the Peace treaties, means, thou shalt hate the people of other nations.**

The solution of these fundamental problems was hammered out by the young Hitler in suffering, and the lessons learnt burnt into his soul. Most men who had endured what he had, would have joined the ranks of those preaching the gospel of hate; hatred of the rich and powerful, and hatred of the peoples of other nations. It is true that in *Mein Kampf*, he shows something of the old Adam, but the fires of suffering have burnt all dross out of his soul, so that he comes today before men with a message of Peace and goodwill.

We have many impressions of Hitler from those who have known him personally, but perhaps the most interesting is the one given by his jailer. The relation of jailer and prisoner is naturally a difficult one, and yet he speaks of Hitler's unfailing courtesy, and prompt recognition of the necessity for prison discipline. The jailer occasionally had difficulties with the young Nazis, who were indignant at their imprisonment, and chafed at prison rules. When trouble arose he had only to go to Hitler, who would say, "leave it to me", and everything was put right. He speaks of his unfailing cheerfulness, how he encouraged his followers, and kept them interested to break the monotony of prison life, and of his invincible courage in spite of the apparent wreckage of his party.

His kindly personality, simplicity, modesty and absence of all pretence are spoken of by everyone. When his old Munich landlady summoned up courage to call upon him, she had only to explain to the two S.S. men on guard that she had known Hitler in the old days, to have every door opened to her and to be greeted by Hitler as a dear old friend.

While Hitler has this charming personality, he is of the stern stuff of which leaders of revolutions are made. He stands apart and like all men of genius who have led great movements he is simple and direct, and puzzles and alarms the complex confused personalities of the ordinary diplomatist; yet anyone who will with an open mind study his speeches and watch his actions can learn to understand him. Dwelling among his beloved mountains he makes his decisions and carries them out swiftly and with absolute certainty.

He burns with one consuming passion, his love of Germany and the German people, rich and poor, old and young, and above all the children. "How wonderful", he has said, "are the children of Germany."

He feels bitterly her wrongs, the Treaty of Versailles and all that followed. The writer of *Mein Kampf* is there today, with its cynical exposure of European statesmanship, and its call for revenge, but he has found a better way. He has realised that the war and the infamous Treaty were symptoms of a deep rooted disease and that Europe must begin anew.

He bases his political creed on an idealised conception of nationality, and of race of which nationality is the flower. God, he tells us, has made different nations. Each nationality has something to contribute to civilisation but the value of the contribution lies in its being essentially national. Those who say that Hitler is out for the conquest of other peoples show a complete misconception of his beliefs. To introduce an alien element by conquest of another country is to injure your own. A race can only reach its highest perfection if it is kept pure, and a nation must work out its own salvation and must care above all else for its own people. Patriotism in its highest form means the complete subjugation of individual gain for the whole community. He believes that no alien element can be expected to work in with this ideal, and herein lies one of his main arguments against the Jewish community in Germany.

Instead of suppressing nationalities, the policy of the treaties which the League supported, he takes that deep emotion - love of country - and bends it to a new purpose, service to one's own people and peace with one's neighbours.

There are times when God in compassion for the self inflicted sufferings of men sends a man simple and direct in thought and inspired by one passion, to carry out an ideal which controls him. Hitler has been entrusted with the task not only of saving the German people, but of securing peace in a distracted Europe. **Future generations will recognise him as the man who led Europe into the paths of peace.**

2

The Beleaguered City

In order to understand Hitler's denunciation of the Treaty of Versailles, it is necessary to realise the strategic position of Germany at the time he came into power, and to compare the map of Europe at that time with the map before the war. Germany is bounded by other countries, except along the Baltic, and if we proceed to trace this post-war frontier we shall find that the title given to this chapter was fully justified at that time.

We shall begin with the frontier facing France. Alsace and Lorraine, which had belonged to Germany since the war of 1870, were restored to France. These territories which contain a mixed French and German population, have changed hands more than once. Louis XIV seized them in time of peace, and they continued to be part of France after the close of the Napoleonic wars, to be regained by Germany in 1870. France never ceased to look forward to their recovery; the statues in Paris representing the two provinces being always draped in black. It is probable that if they had not been taken by Germany in 1870, the war of 1914 would have been confined to Eastern Europe. While the Treaty of Versailles was being drafted, Foch wished to have the whole of the Rhine Provinces added to France, and during their occupation after the Treaty was signed, attempts were made to agitate for their separation from Germany. The plebiscite taken in the Saar at the end of its occupation under the League, showed clearly that these provinces had no desire for separation, but they were included in the neutral zone, and German troops were forbidden to enter them. France built the Maginot line of forts within five miles of the frontier, armed with powerful siege guns able to throw shells twenty miles inside the German frontier. These forts extended from the Rhine to the borders of Luxembourg.

The Treaty of Versailles re-created the country of Poland out of Russian, German and Austrian territory, and in order to give Poland an outlet to the sea, presented her with a broad strip of land on the Vistula, ending in the town of Danzig, which was made a free city under the suzerainty of Poland and the League. This strip of territory cuts off East Prussia from the rest of Germany. Difficulties have arisen over Danzig, the population of which is more than 90% German, difficulties which have been increased by Poland building the new port of Gdynia in the neighbourhood, on Polish territory, to which her sea-going trade is being diverted. The Polish corridor contains a mixed population of Poles and Germans, and was given to Poland without a plebiscite. According to the German census of 1910, it contained a majority of Germans. A considerable section of Silesia, including three quarters of the valuable Silesian coal fields, was given to Poland in spite of a plebiscite in favour of retention by Germany. As this extensive minefield had been developed by German capital, and contained a considerable German population, this region has also been the source of endless difficulties. One of the causes of trouble is the low standard of living and wages of the Polish miner, wages which the German miner who was handed over has had to accept.

The Treaty of Versailles carved up the whole Austrian Empire, creating the new country of Czecho-Slovakia, which contained six different races over whom the Czechs, having a small majority, have ruled. Bohemia which, as can be seen from the map, cuts into the heart of Germany, was formerly part of the friendly Austrian Empire, but now belongs to Czecho-Slovakia. It has been a bone of contention between the Czechs and the Germans for centuries, contains a population one third German and two thirds Czech, and includes the important historical city of Prague. The German population suffered severely under Czech rule; the Czechs never having carried out the clauses in the Peace treaties designed for the protection of minorities. Czecho-Slovakia is a democracy, but a democratic government is no protection to an alien race in a permanent minority, and the Czechs kept their prisons full of German political prisoners.

It is generally admitted today that the commissioners who drew up the new frontiers showed very little wisdom or knowledge of the various peoples whose fate they were deciding in an arbitrary manner. They refused a plebiscite which had been promised by Wilson whenever it suited their purpose.

If we now look at the geographical position of Germany as a whole when Hitler came into power, it is obvious that she had extensive frontiers on the other side of which were peoples who were far from friendly, not through any faults of the German people of today, but because of long enmity extending into the past. France and Germany had been foes since the days of Louis XIV both for racial and historical reasons, and **France hastened, as soon as the war was concluded, to build up an army far more formidable than the one she had possessed in 1914**, to make alliances with Poland and Czecho-Slovakia directed against Germany, and to lend these countries large sums to enable them to buy arms. In Bohemia, in place of the friendly Austrian Empire, Germany had the Czechs who were her hereditary foes, and resuscitated Poland was not too friendly to the Germans who assisted in carving up her territory in the 18th century. Behind Poland and Czecho-Slovakia lies the Soviet Republic which has two reasons for hating Germany: the racial reason that as Slavs they hate Germans; and the political reason that the Soviet is a Communist Government bitterly opposed to National Socialism, the Nazi revolution being just in time to prevent a Communist revolution in Germany. Finally, France, after the signing of the Treaty of Locarno, which seemed to give Germany some security, entered into an alliance with Russia which Czecho-Slovakia also joined. Czecho-Slovakia offered Bohemia to Russia as a base for her bombing planes, within 150 to 250 miles of every important city in Germany except Hamburg, and promised a free passage to the Soviet troops through her territory to attack Germany.

No one therefore who looks at the map can doubt the correctness of the title I have given to this chapter. The huge guns of the Maginot line can destroy the German towns to 20 miles behind the frontier, and it forms a military base for the invasion of the Rhine provinces; while a Russian fleet of bombing planes planted in Bohemia can destroy the cities of Germany. The invasion of the Ruhr by France in time of peace had shown Germany what to expect from her neighbours if she remained in this vulnerable position to the enemy without the gates.

In addition, at the time when Hitler came into power, the Communist vote had risen to 7 million, and the German people had already experienced the horrors of a Communist rising in Munich, Central Germany, the Ruhr Valley and in Hamburg. Horrors that would have been repeated all over Germany if Hitler had not acted promptly. Germany's very existence depended on a highly centralised government; a stern internal discipline; the training to arms of the young men; the possession of munitions not inferior to her neighbours; and the organisation of the whole nation for one purpose, the preservation of the German people from attack. Germany is not in the position to attack, nor desirous of attacking any nation in Europe; but no nation could be expected to tolerate for long this policy of encirclement without taking measures for defence.

3

National Socialism

Before describing National Socialism, it is necessary to discuss the ideas that inspired the political systems of the 19th century, which saw the rapid spread of democratic forms of government originating from the writers of the 18th century. Brought up from childhood in the belief that Democracy was the last word in perfect government I may be allowed to criticize it in my old age.

The stress of the war and the aftermath of war has led not only to the flight of Kings but the collapse of Parliaments and the rise to power of rulers from the people. Dictators govern or non-parliamentary regimes exist in Turkey, Russia, Poland, Germany, Italy and Spain, dictators who have risen to power by the sheer necessity of the situation. The average man, peasant or workman, is not interested in theories of Government. All he asks is law and order and a reasonable modicum of honesty and efficiency. The failure to obtain this minimum has resulted in the rise of Dictators, to replace anarchy and revolution by law and order.

The Government of our country, which has grown up through the centuries and like a patched old coat sits comfortably on the shoulders of John Bull, is not to be taken as a typical example of Democratic Government. Artificially created Democracies are very different.

A Democratic Government gives every adult citizen a vote for the election of a member of Parliament and from among the members of Parliament the Government of the day is chosen. He therefore has a part in the Government and the utmost freedom of opinion is necessarily allowed so that the elector can decide what he wants and vote accordingly.

The defect in Democracy is that while it gives the individual citizen certain powers and privileges it asks nothing from him in return for the benefit of the community. In fact the community has no organized conscious national life. The voter having recorded his vote has no further duties to the State than to keep the law and avoid the police. It is true the citizen may be called upon by the State to fight as a soldier, but in time of peace nothing is asked of him. Parliament may pass laws for the common good but they are administered by State officials. The only organized life with an ethical idea of service is centred round the Churches or voluntary organizations. The Democratic State having given the utmost tolerance to freedom of opinion leaves the citizen to act as best he can for his own aggrandisement. The State consists of separate disconnected units and is not a living organism. It has made a God of Intellect but left out Ethics. It is notorious that in continental Parliaments each Party is willing to sacrifice the common good to its own advancement, and that they are incompetent and apt to become corrupt.

We have been saved from these defects because centuries of tradition have planted in us certain instincts which cause us to regard the body politic as a whole and to pull together in times of crisis in defence of the Nation; but that does not necessarily happen in artificial Democracies.

Our constitution is so complex, with a Monarchy, with a House of Lords, with traditions and customs derived from the past, and with all kinds of influences flowing into the national life, that it cannot be compared with any other Democracy. We have above all traditions of service which come from the Aristocracy and landed classes of this country who, though deprived of power and to a great extent of wealth, still occupy the front pages as news, because of what they stood for in the past, and still in many instances stand for to-day. It is true the new rich and the more frivolous members of the Aristocracy have lowered the standard, but the best of the old families continue quietly their social duties. I can admire an old family who, like the Cecils, through generations have preserved a standard of public service, but I cannot admire a successful soap boiler.

To them we owe the fact that our public schools still carry on that ideal of service - though never expressed - to the State and the Empire, and the ruling classes trained in them still keep control of the government. It is not without interest that just as our public schools with their system of monitors and heads of games and houses are training boys to rule in the best sense of the word, so Hitler has found the need for the same idea in Germany and through the Hitler Youth Organisation is giving that training which is so essential and which has always been absent from the German schools.

The Established Church has also kept up a tradition of Christian conduct, and the Society of Friends has always set a high standard of public service. I remember visiting a linen mill at Belfast many years ago and being horrified to see the girls at the machines in a room full of steam, soaked to the waist, and with no opportunity of changing before going home in the bitter cold outside. I asked: "Are all your mills like this?" "All but one", was the reply, "but", with a shrug of the shoulders, "that belongs to a Quaker".

We can call our constitution a Democracy if we like, but it is modified by traditions drawn from the past which make it workable. All these traditions of national life are necessarily absent in Germany, because of her history, and have to be created.

We have another advantage owing to the fact that a stable though changing form of Government has existed so long in this country. Like pebbles in a stream, we have rubbed together until we are rounded and trained in toleration and moderation.

It was the absence of any idea of the State as an organized whole that led the thinkers of the 18th and early 19th century to try to plan a State in which the individual served the community. If by Socialism we mean the idea of the State as an organic whole to which the individual members must render service, it is as old as Plato's Republic, and certain early writers on Socialism, and Hegel in his Political Philosophy, developed this conception.

Democracy combined with the false interpretation of the Economics of Adam Smith into a rule of conduct, had reduced the people of this country to such a condition by the middle of the 19th century that if the State had not interfered by legislation, we would have committed race suicide! Unfortunately for the advance of civilized communities Karl Marx, by means of an unsound economic theory, sidetracked the Socialist movement from its purpose of remodelling the whole State, into a class war by which the Proletariat was to seize all the means of production and eliminate the middle class. The movement towards a true Socialistic development of the State which we owe to Ruskin, Owen, Kinglery, and Disraeli, was directed into a class war which has produced red revolution in Russia and been barren of any productive results in this country. Social legislation has been passed by both the Conservative and Liberal parties, but since a separate Labour Party was formed, though twice in office, they have produced no results, the last progressive piece of legislation - the Housing and Unemployment Acts - having been passed by the Coalition Government under Lloyd George. The attempts to create a class party and a class war in this country have proved a failure.

The people of this country, tired of political strife, have now twice returned by large majorities a Coalition Government, not because they necessarily admire its capacity or efficiency but because they are determined not to trust the country or the Empire to those who lead the Labour Party and still mumble the ideas derived from Karl Marx. The Bovril of Communism mixed with luke warm water does not attract the majority of voters. The complaint is made that the youth of the country takes no interest in politics. They have too much sense.

The time has come when we must return to Plato and the conception of the State as an organic whole to which each citizen must give service, and the sacrifice of individual interests for the common good.

THE CASE FOR GERMANY.

We must remember that we profess Christianity and that the principles governing the relations of the individual to his fellows have been laid down for all time in the Gospels, and given us the right ideals on which to found a living organic State. This does not mean that we have to deny Democracy, but on the contrary endow Democracy with an ethical principle. We are not wanting as a community in ethical instincts and desire to benefit our fellow creatures, but the whole needs co-ordinating as a conscious ethic guiding the Government and the individual. Without such an ethic, Democracy demoralizes the politician and the Press. We need therefore to return to a genuine Socialism, that is, the conception of the State as an organic living entity demanding service and sacrifice of individual gain from its members, and ending class war and spoliation.

There are times in history when a great leader arises and sweeping aside all forms of Government establishes a personal rule. Such a crisis had arisen in Germany, and Hitler has become a great leader, but the main interest to the student is not his personal rule but the ideal of a State which he has evolved and is working out in Germany.

He is the product of all those, from Plato onwards, who have imagined the State as an organic whole consciously guided by an ethical principle and calling on its individual members to play their part each in his place in helping forward the ethical idea by which the State is guided. His originality lies in converting these abstract ideas into a living principle of life by substituting for the abstraction the State, the living reality - the German Nation.

The sufferings of the German people have made them ardent Nationalists. The Fatherland, crushed and trampled on by the Nations of Europe, suffering every humiliation, has become to the German people the one object of their devotion. The love of the Reich has become a living and consuming flame. Hitler has seized upon that and directed it to an ethical aim. If we wish to appeal to youth we must ask them for service and if need be sacrifice. Only in that way can we utilize their ethical inspiration, and so he has appealed to the youth of Germany. He

| 23 |

will accept no class division; he will stamp out all class war. No man can ask more than to be a citizen of the German Nation, and it is as a member of the body corporate that Hitler addresses his appeal to him.

He has fused all parties together to cast them in a new mould. He has accepted the economic system of Germany as he found it, though he is modifying it in many ways by the action of the State, and while he has carried out many sound reforms profoundly modifying conditions in Germany, these are merely the outward and visible sign. He is aiming at a change of heart, a new ideal of action, a conversion of the German people, without which external machinery is of little use. Doubtless many of the experiments will fail and fresh plans be worked out, but as long as the ethical idea is there, reforms are easy which here would be difficult.

It must be remembered that the Continental Trades Unions are very different to ours, being almost entirely in the hands of political agitators. Obviously the existence of Trades Unions whose leaders were paid to promote class war, was intolerable to the Nazi idea, and Hitler substituted the organization called the Labour Front, with committees of masters and men elected by secret ballot, and State officials who act as overseers and have the last word. Most elaborate labour laws have been passed guarding the workman in every kind of way, and while wages are low the conditions of life are very much improved. Not only are full wages paid during all holidays but the "Strength through Joy" organization has brought to every workman the opportunity of attending concerts and theatres and of cheap holiday travel including sea voyages and visits to foreign countries. Two special 25,000 ton ships have been built and four others chartered for this purpose, and hiking hostels are provided everywhere.

Housing is being carried out on an enormous scale, both in town and country, and factories are not only being made sanitary but pleasant to work in with the provision of dining rooms and bathing facilities. There is still much distress in big cities and the most complete and remarkable

THE CASE FOR GERMANY.

voluntary association has been created to deal with this problem, while the "one pot meal" every month during winter has helped to provide funds. It may be truthfully said that in Berlin last winter no person went without sufficient food and clothing and enough coal to keep one fire burning. The Nazi organization puts at the service of the State a million and a half willing voluntary workers.

Hitler has said that a healthy State is built on the peasant, and Germany has over half a million peasant families cultivating their own land. Our peasants alas are landless. He has made the house and land the possession of the family for all time descending from father to son, and has made it illegal to mortgage the house and farm. Any destitute member of the family has the right to food and shelter in the ancestral home. Prices are fixed and the State organizes distribution. Good food is cheap and plentiful in Germany, yet the peasant is doing well. The middle man is retained for distribution but can no longer rig the market and ruin the farmer with low prices, and plunder the consumer.

The only way the traveller can judge internal prices is by what he pays in restaurants. Two of us made an excellent meal on roast venison with cranberry sauce, Swiss cheese, butter, brown bread and beer for a total of three and a half marks in Nuremberg.

When Hitler first got control there were six million unemployed in Germany. To-day there is a shortage of workmen, and Italian, Dutch and Polish workmen are being, brought in. Those for whom work could not be found during the first years were employed in road making, land reclamation and similar tasks. They had to move from place to place and so live in camp, and were necessarily under discipline to ensure order and train them to a form of labour which was new to many of them. Our plan of paying men the dole and allowing them to loaf in idleness is utterly abhorrent to the German mind. The employment of the unemployed on public works in this country was destroyed by the Trades Unions demanding standard rates of wages for unskilled labour. The cost was prohibitive. Clothed, fed and housed, and his family looked after, the German unemployed are glad to work. This has been described by our Labour Party as slave labour. No one would be more astonished than the German unemployed at such a description.

I shall deal in more detail with parts of this social re-organization in subsequent chapters, but I have said enough to show the general lines. They will make mistakes; but the team spirit is there and the determination to succeed. Our Policy under the false application of the teaching of Adam Smith was in the 19th century to put economic gain first. Hitler's policy has been to put the well being of the people first, to consider the race not the multiplication of goods. He has been rewarded by success in the field of economics.

Nothing has caused more criticism of the German revolution than their handling of the Jewish question. I do not propose to defend it, but give certain explanations which are worthy of consideration. It is perhaps unnecessary to say that the whole business has been grossly exaggerated and active imaginations have been at work inventing unspeakable horrors. During the early days of the revolution brutalities were committed on both sides, many of Hitler's followers being shot down by Communists, and rightly or wrongly they hold in Germany that Communism is a Jewish revolutionary movement.

The hatred of the Jew on the continent is not confined to Germany. The anti-Jewish pogroms that have taken place in Poland were so dreadful that the Polish Government did not allow any news of them to leave the country, and there can be no doubt that Hitler, by bringing the whole matter under law and regulation, saved the Jews from massacre. It is difficult for us to understand this bitter hatred. We find the Jew a law-abiding, hard-working citizen, and have no complaint to make. It is doubtless true of the Jew as of all human beings, that good treatment makes a good citizen and bad treatment a bad citizen.

The only law passed by the Government dealing with the Jewish question, when Hitler came into power, was the Nuremberg Law dealing with marriage. There are to-day some 500,000 Jews in Germany but they are excluded from many professions and Government service.

THE CASE FOR GERMANY.

On the other hand they have their own cultural society, theatres and concerts and are protected from ill treatment by the Police.

Mixed up with this Jewish question is the racial question. The Nordic peoples differ from the Latin peoples in guarding jealously the purity of the blood. We have never in this country objected to inter-mixed marriages with Jews, but an officer in the army in India who marries a Hindu girl would have to resign his commission, while in the U.S.A. and South Africa etc. the slightest taint of negro blood means social ostracism.

In dealing with this difficult question I merely wish to point out that enmity to the Jew is not peculiar to Germany, and that it is better to regulate the Jewish position by law than to have outbreaks of fanaticism. True, Karl Marx was a Jew and rightly or wrongly, as I have said, Communism is regarded in Germany as being Jewish in origin and being organized by Jews.

The dismissal from their posts of distinguished men of learning, artists, musicians, scholars and men of science because they were of Jewish blood gave great offence among the intellectual classes. Art, science and learning recognizes no boundaries of race. What was not known in this country was that these men were offered full retiring pensions if they remained in Germany and that they had managed to fill a large preponderance of posts to the exclusion of Germans. It is true that our Government is doing its best to-day to exclude foreign musicians and actors from this country, a most indefensible proceeding which makes it difficult to criticize the action of Germany, but it was the dismissal given in the highest ranks of learning that shocked Europe and America. Every revolutionary political movement like every religious movement has its excesses and intolerances, and far too much has been made of their blunders. To-day we regard the French Revolution with all its horrors and excesses as marking a step forward in political history. It is only necessary to look back at contemporary writing in this country to realize we could not see the wood for the trees.

The quarrel with Rome was inevitable, because the Vatican will interfere in politics, and just as we had to fight the Vatican to a finish for two hundred years, so any strong Government which wishes to be master in its own home has sooner or later to face the opposition of Rome. We at any rate should understand and sympathize with the position of the German Government.

To us the whole idea of imprisonment for political opinions is abhorrent, but we do not hesitate to arrest and imprison thousands of prisoners without trial in India, and in Belfast to-day any Roman Catholic is liable to arrest and trial before a secret tribunal and can be imprisoned merely on "suspicion" without trial. Political prisoners are not peculiar to Germany. All continental countries, including Democratic Czecho-Slovakia and even France have their political prisoners and secret police.

4

The Nazi Rallys at Nuremberg

Once a year, early in September, all eyes in Germany are turned to Nuremberg. The world at large takes an ever greater interest in this city as the years go by. It is here where the National Socialist Party holds its annual rallys. These are gatherings entirely different to similar events in the parliamentary democracies. The difference is not only to be found in the huge assemblies of the SA and SS men, the corps of political leaders, the Hitler Youth and the Labour Service but, at each gathering, the Führer lays down his programme of work for the coming year. The names given to these annual rallys are also characteristic. "The Victory of Faith", the "Triumph of Will", were the first two after the assumption of power. Early this year, the Führer had already assigned the title of "Rally of Peace" to the 1939 gathering.

I will endeavour to describe the impressions gained when in September 1937 I was given the opportunity of attending that rally.

As I sped towards the old city of Nuremberg, I tried to remember it as I had seen it many years ago, a perfect specimen of mediaeval Germany surrounded by its old walls and towers. How would the venerable city take to playing its part as the Mecca of the new revolution that was transforming Germany? Of one thing I was sure, that the German people under their new leader, with his sense of the artistic and his love of everything German, would not have done anything to desecrate this priceless treasure from the past.

There is a new Nuremberg, for Nuremberg is today, as it was in the middle ages, an important manufacturing centre; but it lies outside the city walls, and not even the railway has been allowed to enter and to spoil the old town. On leaving the station, the old walls are facing you looking like an illustration from Grimm's fairy tales. On the day of my arrival the battlements were decorated with the long red banners with a white disc and the black swastika in the centre, which Hitler designed for his party and which is now the flag of Germany. Beautiful in colour, the long banners draped the old grey walls, in perfect harmony, and they seemed pleased with this new decoration. It was of good omen, that the new revolution was so closely knit with the past of the German people and was not a garish and vulgar twentieth century invention. Hitler had not only chosen Nuremberg as the Mecca of the Nazi party because its people had been faithful to him in the early days of the movement, but also because he wanted to associate the revolution indelibly in the German mind with the past.

Walking through the streets of Nuremberg I saw only two varieties of decoration. The green branches of the pine, and the long red banners hung everywhere. Those who saw the decoration of Bond Street at the time of the Coronation will get some idea of the general effect.

The streets were crowded with people, and with the men of the S.A. in their brown uniforms, and the S.S. in their black uniforms, who had special charge of the crowd. No soldiers and hardly any police were visible anywhere. I was amused to read in an English newspaper from their special correspondent at Nuremberg that the streets were swarming with soldiers.

It so happened that I was so fortunate as to step out of the station just when the Führer was expected to pass by on his arrival. Both sides of the street were lined with a jolly crowd joking and laughing with the S.S. men in their black uniforms, to whom had been given the task of holding them back. They stood about a yard apart with a leather band held between them to form the barrier, and with no weapon of any kind except a small dagger. There could be no question that it was a joyous

THE CASE FOR GERMANY.

crowd looking well fed. One day I mentioned to a working woman in this country that under the Nazi regime the German people were only allowed a quarter of a pound of butter a week each. She stared at me in astonishment and said "I have not eaten butter for years, I cannot afford it".

Presently as I stood waiting, some open cars went by containing Nazi officials who were duly cheered. Then there was a long pause which was broken by the passage of a motor bicycle belonging to the police, with a yellow flag which passed by to see that the road was clear, and then we heard the roar of *"Heils!"* in the distance coming nearer and nearer. The excitement of the crowd was infectious, at last I was to see the Führer, the man who held Germany in the hollow of his hand and commanded respect in Europe. His solitary open car moving at about six miles an hour, accompanied with no escort, was approaching. Standing in the car beside the driver was a slim erect figure in brown uniform, with one hand resting on the windscreen and the other arm held out in the Nazi salute. He looked straight in front, his face serious and composed. We are accustomed in our processions to the smiles and bows of Royalty, but I imagine the immovable erect figure is derived from the tradition of the old Roman Generals when receiving a triumph.

I had read in our newspapers that Hitler never dared to move outside unless he was surrounded by an armed guard. Not only was he alone, but the S.S. men lining the street had no weapon to protect him. But what of Hitler himself? I saw him many times afterwards talking with the officers of the S.S. and S.A. and speaking in the stadium, and tried to compare him with other great men I have seen in my life, men of strong personality as all such men must be. No man cares less for the display of power. When he received the march past of the S.A. and S.S. men in the old market square, he was dressed in a brown shirt, riding breeches and black riding boots without hat or coat. We are used to a display of gorgeousness on the part of generals riding on a charger wearing a magnificent uniform and covered with medals. Hitler's uniform did not differ from that worn by his S.A. men, and his only decoration was the decoration for valour - the Iron Cross of the First Class. It seemed inconceivable that this man in the brown shirt talking with his officers was the master of Germany.

His face is familiar to all of us from his photographs but they do not do him justice. I have never seen one that I liked; he eludes the camera which does not register what is most of interest in his face and expression. He is different to any man I have ever seen before. A flame seems to burn within that slim figure and to look out of his eyes. There is nothing of the fanatic in his expression, but a look of superhuman energy and intensity of purpose; the face of a man specially endowed with the capacity for power; his very simplicity and absence of ostentation strengthens the impression. Bonaparte for all his genius was a vulgar soul and clothed himself in Imperial robes and troubled himself about the details and the etiquette of a court. Such trivialities are impossible for Hitler. Studying his face we can understand those quick decisions which have astonished his followers and electrified Europe; decisions carried out with a surprising rapidity and efficiency. Like Bonaparte he is always in advance of other people and therefore takes them by surprise. Bonaparte had a habit much disliked by the opposing generals of arriving with his army twenty four hours before it was possible for the army to be there; if Hitler had the vulgar ambition for military conquest, he would be the most dangerous man in Europe to-day, because he would outmanoeuvre the generals, just as he has outmanoeuvred the diplomatists by the simplicity and directness of his approach to all questions; but he belongs to a new age in which such conquests are an anachronism, though the diplomatists of Europe living still in the past have not yet realised that fact, and therefore pile up armaments which compel Germany to do the same in self-defence.

I have not yet begun to tell what I saw in Nuremberg and the impression it made upon me, but in truth there is only one man in Nuremberg amid all these crowds - the Führer.

Everywhere one met with friendly faces and a charming welcome. The Germans are probably the only people in Europe who really like

THE CASE FOR GERMANY.

us, and admire us probably much more than we deserve. It is because of that very liking that when irritated by the attacks in our press, and by our public men, they at last turn on us and give us some of our own back again. Attlee speaking in the House of Commons calls Hitler a gangster, and a German newspaper accuses Baldwin of bawling like a street urchin. It is all very childish and stupid. As I have said, they like and admire us, and I defy anyone not to like them. We feel at home with them as we can never feel with a Frenchman or an Italian. I myself am a Scotsman, and it is perhaps truer to say that the Scotsman and the German always get on well together.

The three things which impressed me most during my stay in Nuremberg were the torchlight procession, winding through the streets, the long red banners glowing in the light from the torches; the meeting of the Politische Leiter in the great stadium at night; and the parade of the boys of the labour camps.

This is the part of the Nazi organisation which has attracted most attention in this country. Started on a voluntary basis before Hitler came into power, he at once realised its importance in training the youth of Germany to the idea of citizenship taught by the Nazi party, and its significance as symbolising the whole Nazi conception of the State.

At about 19 years of age every boy in Germany, whether he be rich or poor, "Cook's son, Duke's son, Son of a belted Earl", spends six months in a Labour camp with spade and pick reclaiming the waste soil of Germany to make it fit for cultivation, draining the land, improving the forests, planting trees, and doing all that is needed to develop the natural resources of Germany. They all live and work together, and so that there shall be no distinction between rich and poor, they are all limited to the same amount of pocket money, and like the English school boy the hamper from home is shared with everybody.

The fundamental ideas of National Socialism are all expressed in this organisation. The dignity of Labour, even of the roughest kind, if undertaken in the service of the Reich; the wiping out of the distinction between the bourgeoisie and the workman; and the union of the

German people as members one with another. Incidentally it is giving Germany the most physically fit youth in the world.

Every year contingents are sent from every part of Germany to be received by Hitler in the great stadium at Nuremberg; they are all in a uniform of their own with their knapsacks on their backs, and shouldering a brightly polished spade instead of a rifle. Each contingent has its own band and carries its own banners, the swastika banner, having on it a spade surrounded by a wreath of corn *[Scriptorium: actually, wheat]*. The stadium was packed with people when Hitler arrived; then we heard the music of the band of the first contingent and as they marched we all rose and saluted the flag. On passing Hitler they broke into the goose step, and then turning to the left, the spades flashing in the sun like mirrors, came in from the back of the stadium and formed up placing their knapsacks on the ground and seating themselves upon them. Contingent followed contingent, until the vast floor of the stadium was filled, then standing up they went through the military salute with the spade instead of the rifle, and stood at ease with both hands resting on the handle of the spade. All these movements were carried out by each section at the word of command with military precision; as the one hand came down upon the other on the spade handle, it rang out as one clap. The neatness with which they performed all these movements was repeatedly applauded by the audience, whose enthusiasm and interest in the boys made me think of a collection of British parents at a school cricket match. The uniforms, the bands, the banners, and the absolute precision of movement on word of command are all intended to show that the glamour which surrounds preparations for war can equally well surround service in the cause of peace. Before dispersing the boys chanted a litany of dedication to the Reich, and in memory of the dead of the great war, written by themselves. Hitler in his speech said that this was the greatest demonstration for peace which the world had ever seen. When he said *"Ein Volk, Ein Reich, Eine Gemeinschaft, Eine Kraft"*, the whole audience rose and thundered applause.

Later in the day I saw some of these boys, brown and sturdy, marching back to camp, singing as they went. The streets were lined with people laughing, cheering and throwing flowers and packets of sweets. As I watched them I could not help thinking of the pale-faced, underfed and underdeveloped boy in our great cities, loafing at a street corner with a fag in his mouth. These German boys, though doubtless full of fun on occasions, have serious faces, inspired by an ideal of service to their fatherland, and ready if necessary to die in her defence. The Führer is their hero.

My last vivid memory is of what took place at the meeting at night in the stadium when Hitler addressed the Politische Leiter. We were sitting in darkness, when suddenly shafts of light shot up all round the stadium, meeting over our heads and forming a temple of luminous pillars symbolising the Reich. Then a soft light fell on the back of the stadium, and we saw, rising into sight, descending the steps, and moving slowly between the ranks massed on the ground, men carrying the long red Nazi banners, the spear points of the poles glancing in the light. Very slowly they moved towards the front of the stadium, symbolising the flow of the life stream of the German people, the audience observing an absolute silence. When they had come to rest, we all rose and sang *Deutschland über alles* and the *Horst Wessel song*. Then the trumpets sounded and Hitler began his speech.

In one part of the stadium was a tragic little group, Austrians, exiled from their land because of their political beliefs, who greeted Hitler with cries of *"Österreich grüßt den Führer"*. One day standing in the street, I found myself next to an Austrian lady. Among the laughing crowds she was silent, her eyes filled with tears. She turned to me and said in English, "I have never seen the Führer before - I think my heart is breaking".

5

The Foreign Policy of Germany

Reply of Mr. Montague Norman to a Reuter representative:
"There will be no sensations except those you invent."

Before explaining the foreign policy of Germany it is necessary to describe briefly the mental attitude of the Nations of Europe towards each other, as expressed by their Press and their politicians, - an attitude that has been clearly revealed by all that has happened in connection with the Spanish civil war. This civil war has inevitably resulted in different nations taking sides, Germany and Italy supporting Franco, and Russia and France the Government in Madrid, while in this country both sides are represented. From the beginning of the civil war armament manufacturers in all countries have been busy supplying munitions to both sides. In addition to munitions thousands of volunteers have poured into the country, more especially from Italy where the people and the Government are both violently pro-Franco. Our Government, by setting up the non-intervention committee have tried to restrain the flood of armaments.

Germany was the first to propose that all Governments pledge themselves to restrain to the best of their ability the entrance into Spain of volunteers, and after considerable delay the non-intervention committee adopted that policy.

THE CASE FOR GERMANY.

Since the date when that pledge was given both Germany and Italy have been repeatedly accused by the French and English Press and by prominent politicians, of having broken faith in this matter, on no evidence except the excited statements of the Madrid Government, and the rumours collected and transmitted as facts by the journalists.

The most outrageous statements have been published, from the accusation that the bombing raid on Guernica was ordered from Berlin, to the accusation by Litvinoff that the Italian Government were responsible for the pirate submarines.

Anything in the way of unreliable rumours can be excused to the Madrid Government, suffering from war hysteria, but the accusations in our Press and by prominent politicians are a different matter.

Let us probe a little deeper into this mental attitude of distrust. France has busied herself making "mutual security" Pacts and lending large sums for the purchase of arms to various nations, so as to secure an overwhelming combination of force directed against Germany. The assumption underlying this policy is that owing to the rapacious instincts of Germany, Peace can only be kept by the threat of war, and by collecting on one side the biggest battalions. Our military alliance with France is made on the assumption that the German Nation is ready at any moment to make an unprovoked aggressive attack on France, an action of which the German Nation has never been guilty.

The same atavistic conceptions of the relations between nations is to be found in the League Covenant itself. In that Covenant the Nations solemnly pledge themselves to refer disputes to the League and accept the League's decision, and even if this prove impossible, to delay war for so many months. Yet in Articles 10 - 16 it is assumed that the responsible Governments of these Nations are capable at any time of making unprovoked attacks on each other and therefore according to the suppositions of the League Policy, Peace can only be preserved among these treacherous ruffians by organizing under the League an overwhelming military force composed of a similar collection of scoundrels.

If the members of the League cannot be trusted, the mutual security pacts are worthless, as all agreements and arrangements between people or nations with the mentality of crooks is unreliable.

I do not propose to be led here into a discussion of the complex and highly disputatious question of Japan in Manchuria and Italy in Abyssinia, but in so far as Europe is concerned, since the formation of the League of Nations only three cases of unprovoked aggression have taken place in Europe, - the seizure of Vilna by Poland, of Memel by Lithuania and the occupation of the Ruhr by France.

That wars may arise in Europe is quite possible. The Treaties of Versailles and Trianon have sown the seeds of numerous wars, but the first step towards Peace is that Nations should accept and believe the honest intention and desire for Peace and for fair play of other nations. That we have departed so far from this reasonable attitude is not due to the peoples of Europe, but to their Press and their politicians.

If I print in a newspaper that Mr. Jones is a liar and a treacherous scoundrel Mr. Jones is able to bring an action for libel, but there is no law of libel for Nations or the rulers of Nations, and the most that can be done is for the aggrieved Government to demand an apology. When a very distinguished politician calls Hitler a gangster in the House of Commons there is no redress.

Evil speaking, lying and slandering is specially forbidden in the Prayer Book but apparently it does not apply to Nations or the Governments of Nations. When M. Blum made a speech while still Prime Minister, in which he promised Czechoslovakia that in case of an unprovoked aggression by Germany, France would declare war, he assumed that an unprovoked aggression was just the kind of thing that Germany would indulge in. We have been told in the French Press that Germany intends to make war on Czechoslovakia, that next spring she intends to attack France, that she is preparing for war against Russia to conquer and annex the Ukraine.

I have discussed this mental attitude at some length because it is so universal that it is assumed as a matter of course, and the grossest insults

THE CASE FOR GERMANY.

against a friendly Power are allowed in Parliament with no protest from our minister of foreign affairs.

In discussing, therefore, the foreign policy of Germany, I am handicapped by the reply that Hitler in his speeches is telling lies to deceive Europe. It is no use stating that his foreign policy is thoroughly understood and accepted by the German people. The reply is that they are ordered with the dread of imprisonment to deceive foreigners, and quotations torn from the context and taken from *Mein Kampf* are given as proof of their duplicity. No one in Germany, including Hitler himself, regards the extreme foreign policy in *Mein Kampf* as a guide to German foreign policy to-day.

Let me in spite of these disadvantages do my best to explain.

We have seen that the Nazi movement is one welding the German people into a living organic State developing their own nationality and culture.

From this devotion to their own nationality comes a respect for other nations. Hitler expressed the faith within him when he said God has created different nations that each should fulfil its own life and culture as its contribution to civilization. He therefore regards the conquest of another Nation as a crime against the national idea, and territory so acquired as a source of weakness to the conquering Nation, because alien elements are introduced into the national life and the conquered people have to be held in subjection, thus destroying their right to fulfil their own national life. He points out that Europe has been engaged for centuries in territorial conquests and in the end the nations have retained their original boundaries.

He regards war for territorial conquest in Europe as a crime against civilization and a useless and unwise expenditure of force. I believe that if Alsace and Lorraine were offered to Germany as a gift she would refuse. He therefore quite truthfully says he cannot conceive of any possible cause for quarrel with France.

On the other hand the German Nation is intensely interested in the conditions under which Germans are living under alien rule, and it has

| 39 |

long been obvious that the Germans in Austria and the Germans in the Sudeten German area would ultimately become members of the Reich. Wherever Germans are living they wish them to become converted to the Nazi conception of a State, but that does not mean disloyalty to the people among whom they dwell. On the contrary it will make them better citizens. There is nothing aggressive towards other Nations in the Nazi faith, and many passages in *Mein Kampf* have been misunderstood because Hitler is discussing the German people in alien lands.

This conception of the true attitude of the German Nation to other Nations is thoroughly understood in Germany. If we examine the foreign policy of Germany, we find this new conception running through their political action. **Hitler has introduced a new idea of the relations between countries in his Peace Pacts, a Treaty between two neighbouring States not to make war on each other for a term of years. This Treaty contains no obligations to act as allies against other Nations. It is the only genuine Peace Treaty ever suggested, all other Treaties being alliances for purposes of war.** This idea is transforming the whole political situation in Europe.

Germany will never sign again a Treaty like the Treaty of Locarno which pledged the members to war under certain circumstances, nor join the League of Nations while Article 16 is operative. She alone of all Nations in Europe is free from obligations to make war under certain circumstances. The extent to which we are committed no citizen of this country knows.

Germany has offered these Peace Pacts to all her neighbours including ourselves. In addition Germany has agreed to a navy only one third the size of ours, and has pledged herself to respect the neutrality of Holland, Belgium and Switzerland. She has established very friendly relations with Italy as they both dread the spread of revolutionary Communism, but she will form no Treaty or Alliance involving possibilities of war.

Germany is very far removed in her mentality from a Pacifist policy. She believes in armed national defence and quick reprisals to an outrage like the bombing of the "Deutschland", but her conception of the right

THE CASE FOR GERMANY.

relations between the Nations of Europe is so new and the mental attitude of the other European politicians towards each other so atavistic that it is a difficult mental gulf for them to cross, and yet it is plain ordinary common sense.

A striking instance of German diplomacy is the agreement that she has made with Belgium. Under the Treaty of Locarno, France and England were pledged to go the assistance of Belgium if attacked, and Belgium was equally obliged to go to their assistance. France and England proposed to Belgium the renewal of the old arrangements but Hitler dropped an explosive bomb into the negotiations by announcing that Germany was prepared to pledge herself to protect the neutrality of Belgium without any conditions. The Belgians being astute diplomatists used this to compel France and England to drop the clause requiring assistance from Belgium in case they were attacked, and France proceeded at once to spend vast sums on a line of forts between herself and her old ally.

The Treaty between Germany and Belgium has now been ratified. Germany pledges herself not only to respect Belgian neutrality but to go to her defence if she is invaded, thus protecting her from an act of aggression by France. As the *Daily Express* says, the new Independence of Belgium is Independence from France.

Germany has entered into the closest relations of friendship with Italy, and Yugoslavia has signed a Peace Pact with Italy and Bulgaria on the German model. Bulgaria has signed a Treaty of Friendship and of arrangement for mutual arbitration with Turkey, and Turkey has signed a Peace Pact on the German model with Persia, Iraq and Afghanistan. We alone have failed to realise the implications of a Peace Pact, and have shown more hostility to Germany since we signed it than we did before.

In none of these Treaties is there a hint of an alliance for purposes of war.

The Pax Germanica now extends from the Channel to the Baltic, from the Baltic to the Mediterranean, and to the frontiers of India.

Ultimately the Peace Pacts will result in the denunciation of the mutual security pacts. Poland having signed a Peace Pact both with Germany and with Russia is getting restive about her mutual security pact with France, which she realises is an obligation that might force her into war against a friendly neighbour.

The great mass of mankind ask for Peace and security abroad, and law, order, and efficient government at home.

Alone among European nations by her home and foreign policy Germany is securing this for the peoples of Europe and therefore the smaller nations are clustering round Germany.

There is another aspect of this question that requires to be dealt with before leaving it.

It is probably true that in 1914 the outbreak of war was very largely due to those in military command in the various countries involved. The last serious war in Europe had been in 1870. It was quickly over, the loss of life was according to our present standards insignificant, and it did not profoundly disturb the economics of Europe or even of France. Those in command of the armies of Europe in 1914 envisaged a war like that of 1870 and if they did not deliberately promote war, did nothing to avert it. After all war is a soldier's business.

To-day the situation is very different. Those in responsible command in Europe dread the idea of war, as they realize from their intimate knowledge what a fearful business it will be. The demand for war comes not from the Totalitarian States, not from the dictator or the soldier, but from the parties of the left in the Western Democracies. The whole policy of France was formerly directed to the oppression of Germany and the creation of a divided Europe, and the danger of France setting fire to Europe was much increased by having a party of the left in power including the Communists.

Daladier had to break with the Communists before he could get his Peace Pact signed.

Athens we know was forced into the Syracusan war by the mob, and to-day it is the parties of the left who are always clamouring for

THE CASE FOR GERMANY.

war. They work themselves into a state of hysteria over the sensational, unverified and one-sided statements published by the Press, and pass resolutions at public meetings urging war on the Government.

At the end of the Abyssinian campaign I was present at a meeting of the Council of Action with Mr. Lloyd George in the chair, a body which consists of Nonconformists and Liberals. They carried a resolution with one dissentient vote, which I gave, in favour of a blockade of the Suez Canal and the Red Sea by our fleet. This would not only have meant war with Italy but as Italy was already in possession of Abyssinia, would have meant serious complications with other Powers including the U.S.A.

At a meeting of the Labour Party not long ago they carried a resolution in favour of our expenditure on armaments because, the leaders explained, if returned to power they would require these armaments to make aggressive war on nations like Germany whose form of Government they did not approve, or undertake ventures like attacking Italy or Japan.

The absurdity of their attitude towards the use of bombing planes by Japan is that we are building a huge fleet of bombing planes to use in exactly the same way if there is war in Europe, the proposals of Germany to limit the use of bombing planes to the actual battle areas having been rejected or at any rate ignored by our Government.

As General Goering said when addressing the war veterans, **"I believe that those who rattle the sabres have not participated in war."**

In pre-war days we used to complain of the German Emperor rattling the sabre. **To-day the rattling is done by the Labour leaders in England, and the real danger of war in Europe would be the success of the Labour Party in a general election. While pretending to be in favour of peace they are the firebrands that might set Europe alight.**

It is madness to have the mob of the left attacking and insulting Nation after Nation in public meetings, and our foreign office entering into commitments in Europe unless we are prepared at once to introduce conscription. We sent our half trained boys to fight trained soldiers in 1914 with the result that in the war of attrition that Earl Haig was always talking about three English soldiers were killed for one German. Is the same slaughter of our youth to take place again? Why can we not go quietly about our lawful occasions and leave other Nations alone?

6

England and Germany

In regard to Anglo-German relationship there has existed no reason for complaint during the last twenty years. The Germans have made a number of approaches with a view to stablishing a better and closer understanding but all without avail. There is no evidence to show that these German approaches were not made honestly and fairly. I will quote only two examples from a number of such statements. The first is the relative passage in the Führer's speech of April 28, 1939, when he stated:

> "During the whole of my political activity I have always expounded the idea of a close friendship and collaboration between Germany and England. In my Movement I found innumerable others of like mind. Perhaps they joined me because of my attitude in this matter. This desire for Anglo-German friendship and cooperation conforms not merely with sentiments which result from the racial origins of our two peoples, but also to my realization of the importance for the whole of mankind of the existence of the British Empire. I have never left room for any doubt of my belief that existence of this Empire is an inestimable factor of value for the whole of human cultural and economic life. By whatever means Great Britain has acquired her colonial territories - and I know that they were those of force and often

brutality - nevertheless I know full well that no other Empire has ever come into being in any other way, and that in the final resort it is not so much the methods that are taken into account in history as success, and not the success of the methods as such, but rather the general good which the methods yield. Now there is no doubt that the Anglo-Saxon people have accomplished immeasurable colonizing work in the world. For this work I have a sincere admiration. The thought of destroying this labour appeared and still appears to me, seen from a higher human point of view, as nothing but the effluence of human wanton destructiveness. However, this sincere respect of mine for this achievement does not mean foregoing the securing of the life of my own people. I regard it as impossible to achieve a lasting friendship between the German and Anglo-Saxon peoples if the other side does not recognize that there are German as well as British interests, that not only is the preservation of the British Empire the meaning and purpose of the lives of Britishers, but also that for Germans the freedom and preservation of the German Reich is their life purpose. A genuine, lasting friendship between these two nations is only conceivable on the basis of mutual regard. The English rule a great Empire. They built up this Empire at a time when the German people were internally weak. Previously Germany had been a great Empire. At one time she ruled the Occident. In bloody struggles and religious dissentions, and as a result of internal political disintegration, this empire declined in power and greatness and finally fell into a deep sleep. But as this old empire appeared to have reached its end, the seeds of its rebirth were springing up. From Brandenburg and Prussia there arose a new Germany, the second Reich, and out of it has grown at last the German People's Reich. And I hope that all English people understand that we do not possess the slightest feeling of inferiority to Britishers. Our historical past is far too great for that!

THE CASE FOR GERMANY.

England has given the world many great men, and Germany no fewer. The severe struggle for the maintainance of the life of our people has in the course of three centuries cost a sacrifice in lives which far exceeds that which other peoples have had to make in asserting their existence.

If Germany, a country that was for ever being attacked, was not able to retain her possessions, but was compelled to sacrifice many of her provinces, this was due only to her political misdevelopment and her impotence as a result thereof. That condition has now been overcome. Therefore we Germans do not feel in the least inferior to the British Nation. Our self-esteem is just as great as that of an Englishman for England. In the history of our people, now of approximately two thousand years standing, there are occasions and actions enough to fill us with sincere pride.

Now if England cannot understand our point of view, thinking perchance she may look upon Germany as a vassal state, then our love and friendly feelings have indeed been wasted on her. We shall not despair or lose heart on that account, but - relying on the consciousness of our own strength and on the strength of our friends - we shall then find ways and means to secure our independence without impairing our dignity.

I have heard the statement of the British Prime Minister to the effect that he is not able to put any trust in German assurances. Under the circumstances I consider it a matter of course that we no longer wish to expect him or the British people to bear the burden of a situation which is only conceivable in an atmosphere of mutual confidence. When Germany became National Socialist and thus paved the way for her national resurrection, in pursuance of my unswerving policy of friendship with England, of my own accord I made the proposal for a voluntary restriction of German naval armaments. That restriction was, however, based on one condition, namely, the will and the conviction that a war between England and Germany would never again be possible. This wish and this conviction is alive in me today."

Secondly, in *Mein Kampf* there are many long references to Great Britain, and all of them are couched in tones of great appreciation. Hitler says that if German statesmen had had sufficient foresight to conclude an alliance with England early in the twentieth century, as Japan did in 1904, there would have been no Great War. Another important mistake made by German diplomats was to underestimate the fighting strength of the British Empire. Britain's total effectives were calculated in the basis of her standing army, a most fatal mistake. In this connexion Hitler writes:

> "The fact that England did not possess a national army proved nothing; for it is not the actual military structure of the moment that matters, but rather the will and determination to use whatever military strength is available.
>
> England has always had the armament which she needed. She always fought with those weapons which were necessary for success. She sent mercenary troops to fight as long as mercenaries sufficed; but she never hesitated to draw heavily and deeply from the best blood of the whole nation when victory could be obtained only by such a sacrifice.
>
> And in every case the fighting spirit, dogged determination, and use of brutal means in conducting military operations have always remained the same.
>
> But in Germany, through the medium of the schools, the Press and the comic papers, an idea of the Englishman was gradually formed which was bound eventually to lead to the worst kind of self-deception. This absurdity slowly but persistently spread into every quarter of German life. The result was an undervaluation for which we have had to pay a heavy penalty.

THE CASE FOR GERMANY.

The delusion was so profound that the Englishman was looked upon as a shrewd business man, but personally a coward even to an incredible degree. Unfortunately, our lofty teachers of professorial history did not bring home to the minds of their pupils the truth that it is not possible to build up such a mighty organisation as the British Empire by mere swindle and fraud.

The few who called attention to that truth were either ignored or silenced. I can vividly recall to mind the astonished looks of my comrades when they found themselves personally face to face for the first time with the Tommies in Flanders. After a few days of fighting the consciousness slowly dawned on our soldiers that those Scotsmen were not like the ones we had seen described and caricatured in the comic papers and mentioned in the *communiqués*."

Soon after the War there was a widespread movement in Europe which had as a leitmotif the liberation of India. On this point Hitler writes in *Mein Kampf*:

"I remember well the childish and incomprehensible hopes which arose suddenly in nationalist circles in the years 1920-21, to the effect that England was just nearing its downfall in India.

A few Asiatic mountebanks, who put themselves forward as 'the champions of Indian Freedom', then began to peregrinate throughout Europe and succeeded in inspiring otherwise quite reasonable people with the fixed notion that the British World Empire, which had its pivot in India, was just about to collapse there. They never realised that their own wish was the father of all these ideas.

Nor did they stop to think how absurd their wishes were. For inasmuch as they expected the end of the British Empire and of England's power to follow the collapse of its dominion over India, they themselves admitted that India was of the most outstanding importance for England.

Now in all likelihood the deep mysteries of this most important problem must have been known not only to the German-National prophets but also to those who had the direction of British history in their hands. It is down right puerile to suppose that in England itself the importance of India for the British Empire was not adequately appreciated. And it is a proof of having learned nothing from the World War and of thoroughly misunderstanding or knowing nothing about Anglo-Saxon determination, when they imagine that England could lose India without first having put forth the last ounce of her strength in the struggle to hold it.

Moreover, it shows how complete is the ignorance prevailing in Germany as to the manner in which the spirit of England permeates and administers her Empire.

England will never lose India unless she admits racial disruption in the machinery of her administration (which at present is entirely out of the question in India), or unless she is overcome by the sword of some powerful enemy. But Indian risings will never bring this about.

We Germans have had sufficient experience to know how hard it is to coerce England. And, apart from all this, I as a German would far rather see India under British domination than under that of any other nation."

7

March 7th 1936, a Most Important Date

Both in Germany and in England accounts have been published of the drafting of the Treaty of Locarno and what happened afterwards up to the fateful day of March 7th 1936. Both parties have quoted selected documents and both have produced a convincing case in favour of quite opposite conclusions. The patriotic Englishman is bound to accept our statement without question and the patriotic German is equally bound to accept the German statement. Germany's opponents will always say that she broke the Treaty of Locarno without justification and without warning. The German reply which is equally convincing is that by signing the Franco-Russian Treaty, France destroyed the Treaty of Locarno, and had full and fair warning of the view Germany took.

These discussions lead nowhere. It surely could not be expected that a rearmed Germany, arriving once more to a proud and free national consciousness, would long tolerate a frontier undefended and lying under the French guns of the Maginot line.

We have only to imagine ourselves to have been defeated by a French coalition, and as a result being forbidden to have any ships of war in the Channel, which was permanently occupied by the French fleet. I fear that whatever treaties we had signed, if we saw the opportunity of a surprise recovery we would take it and always glorify that day though we had broken the most solemn of treaties.

There are situations which collapse almost by a law of nature and ordinary rules and regulations are swept away.

It is evident that the humiliating Treaty of Locarno signed by an unarmed Germany, helpless under an armed France, could not be accepted for all time by an armed Germany, nor would they have tolerated long a ruler or a government that took no steps to occupy the neutral zone.

To appeal to France, Belgium and the League for the right of Germany to defend her own frontiers was useless. I believe the people of this country if appealed to would have responded, but the Foreign Office would have refused and the obedient Press supported them.

To denounce the Treaty of Locarno and announce that on a certain day German troops would march in, inevitably meant war, but what would happen if possession was taken without notice and Europe woke up one morning to an accomplished fact?

The risks of the plan adopted by Hitler were enormous. Only a formal occupation was possible and he could not know how many soldiers France had concealed in her underground forts, while the guns of the forts themselves could cause appalling destruction.

The German army was neither trained nor equipped up to the French standard, and it was known that the French military command had been urging the Government to make a **"preventive war"** on Germany, to annihilate her half trained troops and settle the German question for all time.

To move large masses of troops up to the edge of the neutral zone would have attracted attention, and therefore it had to be a formal occupation with a few thousand men whom France could at once have overwhelmed. The risks were so great that I believe only one man in Germany had the courage to put it in practice - the Führer.

The plan having been decided on it was essential that the utmost secrecy be preserved. If it had leaked out prematurely France would at once have sent troops into the neutral zone. Therefore no preparations

THE CASE FOR GERMANY.

were made for the reception of the troops in the frontier towns. The success with which the secret was kept - which must have been known to hundreds of people - speaks highly for German loyalty and discipline.

The people of the Rhine towns had endured for years the hard rule of the French officers and the black troops. Only in our section of occupation were the people treated with decency and humanity.

That terror was gone, Germany was rearming, the message of hope had been received. National Socialism was triumphant, their boys were being called up proud to be trained to defend their Fatherland, but they still lived in a no man's land, dominated by the French guns and the armies of France that in a few hours could ravage a defenceless people.

The whole situation is so remote from our experience, surrounded by the sea, that it is difficult for us to realize what it meant to live in the undefended territory so recently freed from the troops of France. Across that field, at the end of that road is France, armed France, and we are here defenceless. We can imagine their fear, knowing that concealed in those innocent looking green fields are the colossal siege guns waiting ready to blow to pieces their cities and villages.

Without hope and never free from fear the days drag on and no deliverance comes. What is the Führer doing? Is the watch on our beloved Rhine never to be renewed? And then comes the memorable day to be for all time glorious in German history - the 7th of March. There is the tramp of feet, the gleam of the sun on bayonets, soldiers are coming. Can it be the French? But no they are coming from Germany, we see the Swastika banner. It is impossible, it is unbelievable, they are our soldiers, and that night German sentries looked down once more on the sacred river, the Rhine.

And then after joy came the terror of suspense. What will France do? At any moment we may hear the scream of shells from the Maginot line. At any moment French troops may come harrying, burning, destroying.

I often wonder how Hitler endured those hours. He had thrown down a challenge to all Europe. He had played with the dice such a game with fortune as had never been played in the history of the world before. When Julius Caesar crossed the Rubicon he had his armies with him, but Hitler occupied the neutral zone with a mere handful of men, in face of the French army of 500,000 men on a Peace footing. He won and not one shot was fired, one shot that would have set all Europe in a blaze.

All Germany waited in an awful breathless suspense. Then came the news that France had appealed to the League, and in 24 hours the central point of European politics passed from Paris to Berlin. Hitler had secured the initiative and has held it ever since.

What happened during those hours is still a profound secret, but there can be no question that according to the articles of the Treaty of Locarno Germany had committed an act of **"flagrant aggression"** and if asked by France we were pledged to war. It is also equally certain that if the Baldwin Government had attempted war in such a cause they would have been out of power in a week.

Hitler chose the occasion of the occupation of the neutral zone to make a speech on the Foreign Policy of Germany, and this is the most important state document since the Treaty of Versailles.

The speech which I print as an appendix will be found to be a very broad and statesman-like treatment of the whole situation in Europe.

The definite offers made to France and Great Britain would, if they had been accepted, have secured the peace of Europe. Hitler suggested a neutral zone on both sides of the frontier, and a peace pact between Germany, France and Belgium to be guaranteed by England and Italy, and an air pact to prevent the danger of sudden attacks from the air.

He also offered non-aggression pacts with the states bordering Germany on the east, and stated his willingness to rejoin the League of Nations.

These offers were rejected by the governments of France and Great Britain, our reply being the forming of a military alliance with France against Germany, and the questionnaire.

As none of these offers were accepted, they are no longer binding on Germany, and Germany will not now rejoin the League until it is completely reformed and Article 16 abolished.

The good understanding with the Czechs which Hitler offered has now been accomplished. From the first Hitler has said that he had no quarrel with the Czechs but only with Benes. If Benes had accepted Germany as his natural ally from the beginning, for which there were ample geographical and economic reasons, instead of allying Czecho-Slovakia with France and the Soviets against Germany, the whole history of Czecho-Slovakia would have been different.

8

The Real Enemy of Europe

In the former chapters I have tried to show that Germany is engaged in building up a state on new and original lines which is entirely her own affair, whether we like it or not, has no aggressive designs on any other country and wishes to be left alone to develop her internal economy and external trade. She is also quite willing to continue to pay the salaries of Protestant Pastors and Roman Catholic Priests on condition that they leave politics alone and do not use the pulpit to attack the Government.

This being her policy there seems no reason why other Nations and other ideologies should not have left her alone. She is, it is true, strongly armed but so are her neighbours and they began it.

After the threat of war by both France and Great Britain over the Sudeten German question, which was not the business of either of us, she naturally fortified her French frontier, an essential net of defence. As far as we are concerned as we had fallen far below the standard of other countries it was in an uncertain world, but it is obvious that these armaments are not directed against Germany unless our intention is a war of aggression. Nor is Germany arming against us. She has no cause of quarrel with us and no reason to believe that as long as we have a responsible Government in spite of the continued attacks in our Press and by certain politicians, that she has any reason to fear hostility on

THE CASE FOR GERMANY.

our part. She is not looking towards France and England but is looking across the plains of Poland at a much more dangerous enemy. The Soviet with 2,000,000 men on a Peace footing under arms, spent last year £1,000 millions on additional armaments and has behind her an unlimited supply of man power in Asia.

On the contrary while showing occasional nervousness at our expenditure on armaments, which if a popular front coalition came into power would be directed against her, she realises that all the armed forces of Germany, France, Italy and England may be needed to rescue Europe from an Asiatic invasion more formidable than any of the invasions of the past.

I myself share her confidence in our peaceful intention.

To-day Germany is no longer anxious to keep a watch on the Rhine, but on the Dneiper. The suggestions therefore of a mutual reduction of armaments between France, England and Germany are now out of date though at one time Germany would have considered them. She would rather say keep up your bombing plots and your munitions. They may all be needed to defend European civilisation from going down in a hideous massacre.

It is extraordinary how we shut our eyes to this danger with the horrible example of Spain before us. How we talk about the help given to Franco by Germany and Italy but ignore the help given to the Red Government by the Soviet. While the Nazi form of Government is, as Hitler has said again and again, intended for home consumption, Communism is international and is carrying on an underground agitation throughout the world, and insinuating itself into society and other organisations under various plausible names and disguises, having at its disposal the most formidable secret society in the world, continental Free Masonry, which is a very different affair to our amiable Free Masonry over here, and is revolutionary and anti-Christian.

The centre of the Comintern is Moscow and the Soviet Government gave themselves away when they broke of diplomatic relations with Hungary because she joined the anti-Comintern pact.

One of the cleverest lies put forth by the Communists and accepted over here, is that the anti-Comintern pact is directed against Democracy. It is true Germany resents the continued attacks made upon her in the name of Democracy and occasionally shows up the claims of Democracy to be the one perfect political system, but she has no desire to attack or replace Democracy in any Democratic country by another system. To each country the Government it prefers, is her motto. It is true that there is Nazi agitation in some European countries, because throughout the world many people have been convinced in favour of a Nazi State, but such agitation is not encouraged by the German Government.

Communism is an international movement organising revolution in every country, and it has now been clearly demonstrated that the hideous massacres in Spain of Priests, Monks and Nuns, and the burning of Churches was connived at by the Government of the adventurers in Madrid made up of adventurers who had seized power.

The sustained attack on the German Government and the propagation of lie upon lie through our Press and by means of an endless stream of publications is to be traced back to Communist propaganda.

While active Communist agitation has made little progress in this country, India and Burmah are rotten with Communism and Communism is wishing to set the four Powers at each other's throats. Whenever a step has been made towards agreement it swings back again, through a poisonous propaganda in which the British Press leads.

Certain enmity to Germany is therefore to be expected on the part of Socialists, Extreme Protestants and the Roman Catholic Church. Germany has also another enemy - International Finance, because she will not borrow money outside but is holding up an economic system in which there is no room for the international financier.

If she would only borrow £100,000,000 in the City all our Press would coo like sucking doves and our friendship or hostility to the new Spanish Government will depend on whether she consults the City for money.

THE CASE FOR GERMANY.

All the different sources of hostility are at work, but they do not account for the persistent agitation on which large sums of money are being spent, an agitation for a deliberate purpose, a war in which the four Capitalist States will destroy each other so that a Communist state will be built on the ruins, and the one organised source of this persistent agitation is the Comintern with ample funds behind it in Moscow.

The Japanese war in China is not directed against the independence of China or for the possession of territory. It is war against the Soviet. The complete control of the Soviet over Czechoslovakia has been amply proved. When Hitler said he would if compelled fight his way into Sudeten Germany it was not only to free the Sudeten Germans but to close the open door into Europe for the Soviet armies. As I have already pointed out if we had been so rash as to plunge Europe into war on that question and invite the assistance of the Soviet, Europe would have been doomed. In the strategic position of the mountains of Poland, the guns are now pointed not towards Germany but towards Russia. Hungary in past centuries fought bravely against Asiatic invasion holding the strategic position where the Danube turns abruptly to the east. We cannot trust the Slavonic peoples because of their racial affinity and Benes did his best to organise them against Germany.

If Spain had turned red and we had supported Benes against Germany, the day might already have arrived for which the Soviet is waiting. Everyone who however innocently helps the agitation against Germany is playing for war and the triumph of Communism.

9

Communism versus National Socialism

I have already dealt with the dangerous war propaganda of the Labour Party in this country supported by politicians who do not belong to the Party, but it is necessary to look a little deeper into this matter.

The word Socialism is used with so many different meanings that it is necessary before writing these observations to define in which sense it is used in Germany. The broadest definition is the conception of a State which is a living organic whole, in which the members of the State are inspired and guided by the duty of service to the State as paramount.

That is the meaning given to the word by the German to-day when he describes the German State as a National Socialist State.

The meaning attached to the word by the Communists and the members of our Labour Party who are followers of the Jew Karl Marx, is quite different. By Socialism they mean the ownership of all Capital and administration of production, distribution and exchange by the State, and the elimination of the producer and trader for private profit. The Communist differs from the official Labour Party Leaders, not in his aim but in his method, which is certainly somewhat drastic.

The Communist proposes confiscation of all private Capital, the Labour Party leaders propose to buy out the owner of Capital and property. He is to become a pensioner of the State and will no longer be allowed to use his Capital for private venture, a proposal more soothing to the Capitalist than the firing line. The Socialism of our Labour Party is the Bovril of Communism diluted with luke warm water.

The experiment of running a State on these lines is being tried in Russia to-day, but it is too early to say whether it can be successfully done and whether it improves the conditions of the masses of the people.

I do not propose to discuss the merits and demerits of such a system, in which private enterprise is replaced by a huge bureaucracy, in whatever form it be disguised. I merely wish to point out that such a system is incompatible with Democracy, a free Parliament, and freedom of the individual as we understand it. As we see in Russia to-day such a system results in political trials and the firing squad. The Government cannot and dare not allow the slightest divergence in action or opinion. These political trials are an instructive preliminary to establishing universal suffrage in Russia, and remind me of the Colonel who shot every tenth soldier in a regiment "pour encourager les autres".

The Labour Party has failed to convert the majority of the British people to their economic theory of a State. It is true that by adopting the name the Labour Party, they have swept into their organization the Trades Unions and rely on them as a source of income and so create a class party which is supported by a large minority principally composed of wage earners; but these wage earners are not necessarily followers of Karl Marx and many, while subscribing through their union to the party funds, vote for the Conservative Government. The political issue is therefore confused.

The policy of this country has been and is based on individualism in production and trade, modified in two directions, - protection for the wage earner, and when open unregulated barter has proved inefficient, modification of it by a certain amount of organization and arrangement of prices by the State.

If we turn now to Germany we find that the Germans have completely and utterly repudiated Karl Marx Socialism.

The best proof of this is, that they are building their whole economic system on the peasant proprietor, and doing all they can to conserve and strengthen his position, thus pursuing the opposite policy to the Soviet which tried to abolish the peasant proprietor and convert him into the wage slave of the Communist Government. After a fierce struggle in which millions died of starvation the Soviet have arrived at a grudging compromise in which the peasant is allowed a little land and a small modicum of stock of his own.

The German economic experiments are all on our lines. They have carried the protection of the wage earner much further than we have. They have adopted as universal the organization that we have established in the railways for settling disputes about wages. They have improved on our factory inspectors by appointing state officials who have cognizance of the whole conditions of labour.

In the other province they are bringing in State regulation of prices when they think that free competition has been ruinous to the small producer, injurious to the consumer, and only benefited the middle man with ready Capital at this command.

There is another interesting point in this connection. The German Government is building up in trade, in manufacture, in agriculture, organizations of those engaged in the industry with the minimum of State control, in direct contradiction to Karl Marx Socialist ideas, and preserving in that way the liberty of the producer from too much State interference.

They are following and improving the lines we have always followed, basing the economic State on individual effort.

The result is that their bitterest enemies to-day are the followers of Karl Marx from Moscow to the T.U.C. They attack and misrepresent the Nazi rule on every platform and are ready to plunge Europe and this country into war to crush the economic system adopted by the Nazi Government. As the real issue would not appeal to the public, they raise a false cry of Democracy in danger, while they advocate an economic system which would destroy Democracy.

THE CASE FOR GERMANY.

There need be no quarrel about forms of Goverment between us and Germany. They frankly prefer their own as we frankly prefer ours; but they have no desire to force their opinion on other nations, while our Labour Party are prepared to go to extremes to force their opinion on Germany.

A prominent Labour leader said at a "Peace" meeting the other day that he was willing his son should fight and die to destroy the Nazi rule in Germany.

The aggressive party in Europe to-day is not the Nazi party but the followers of Karl Marx whether they call themselves Communists or Socialists.

This quarrel therefore between the Nazis and the followers of Karl Marx is influencing foreign politics and our foreign relations and involving the possibility of war.

It is therefore necessary for the sober British citizen to regard with suspicion what he reads in the Press in the journalistic world here and abroad.

It would be the very irony of fate if we were dragged into a war to promote Communism abroad when we have rejected it at home.

Passing from internal organization to external politics, we find German foreign policy governed by a revolt against control of the nations by a super State centred at Geneva so that whether we examine their domestic or foreign policy, we find the fundamental principle of freedom, freedom of the individual in his own development, and freedom of the group of individuals (the nation) in its development. These ideas are fundamental and strike much deeper than the form of Government.

Behind the Labour Party in this country is the Comintern carrying on Communist propaganda in every corner of the world. It is therefore necessary for us to recognise what is the real ideological battle which is going on in Europe. It is the battle between Communism on the one hand, which means not only the State ownership of all property, and the crushing of individual enterprise, but the denial of God and the destruction of Christianity; and the idea, on the other hand, of a State built on the right of individual enterprise and ownership of private property which are the foundations on which liberty is built.

The issue has been cleverly falsified by representing the struggle of the two ideologies as a war between Communism and "Capitalism". If by "Capitalism" we mean the right to private ownership of property, then the war is rightly described as being between Communism and "Capitalism," but the word "Capitalism" calls up a vision of a fat financier smoking cigars at five shillings apiece, as he rides to the city in his Rolls Royce.

The establishment of Communism and its maintenance necessitates a ruthless tyranny over the individual. We hear little about Russia from the Labour Party to-day. It is buried under a black cloud through which comes the rattle of the shots from the firing squads. If we had been dragged into war over the quarrel between the Germans and the Czechs we would have fought with Stalin as our ally, and we have rightly drawn back shuddering from such a catastrophe.

The revolution in Spain began with horrible massacres accompanied by bestial cruelty in which it is estimated some 400,000 perished, and the ferocity of the murderers was principally directed against the Church.

Behind the struggle of the Sudeten Germans, the Poles and the Hungarians, for freedom from Czech rule, the real contest was with Communism. When Benes made his treaty with Russia it was hailed by the Comintern as a victory for Communism, and Benes was a favoured guest at Moscow because he had opened the door for the entry of the Soviet armies into the heart of Europe. The first act of the new Government in Czecho-Slovakia, which is as democratic as the former government, has been to break the treaty with the Soviet and suppress the Communists societies. Communism has received its severest. blow since the Soviet Government was defeated by the armies of Poland.

France has oscillated between the policy of friendship with and enmity against Germany according to whether the parties of the right or the left were in power, and the Communist party refused to support

Daladier in his policy of reconciliation with Germany, and organized a general strike to prevent the signing of the Peace Pact, and M. Blum, Communist and leader of the Socialist party, has declared against the Peace Pact with Germany.

The world struggle is not between democratic and totalitarian, forms of government, but between the civilization of Western Europe built on individual liberty of action and the ownership of private property, and a State in which all are wage slaves who, if they fail in their quota of production are shot. The shooting of the brilliant inventor who designed the planes which reached the North Pole, because one of the planes came down, should have filled the civilised world with horror.

The amiable idealists of our Labour Party think they can get the best of both worlds with one foot in the Communist camp and the other in the democratic camp. It cannot be done. It is necessary for the democratic countries to decide on which side they stand. There need be no quarrel between Democracy and National Socialism; we both have the task of saving European civilization from the inroads of Asiatic barbarians inspired by a theory which is fundamentally opposed to our conception of civilization. The vanguard facing Communistic Asia is Germany, sword in hand, protecting Europe.

10

The Union of the German People of Austria and the Sudeten Germans With the German People of the Reich

"Further, it has become self-evident to me that those frontier districts between Czechoslovakia and Germany where the Sudeten population is in an important majority should be given full right of self-determination at once. If some cession is inevitable, as I believe it to be, it is as well that it should be done promptly and without procrastination. There is real danger, even a danger of civil war, in the continuance of a state of uncertainty. Consequently there are very real reasons for a policy of immediate and drastic action. Any kind of plebiscite or referendum would, I believe, be a sheer formality in respect of these predominantly German areas. A very large majority of their inhabitants desire amalgamation with Germany. The inevitable delay involved in taking a plebiscite vote would only serve to excite popular feelings, with perhaps most dangerous results. I consider, therefore, that these frontier districts should at once be transferred from Czechoslovakia to Germany, and, further, that measures for their peaceful transfer, including the provision of safeguards for the population during the transfer period, should be arranged forthwith by agreement between the two Governments."

(Vide: Runciman Report No. 7, 1938.)

The rise of the Austrian people in rebellion against Schuschnigg in a few hours, the fall of Schuschnigg from power, the telegram from Dr. Seyss-Inquart, the head of the new government, to Hitler to send troops to preserve order, the triumphant march of the soldiers of the Reich into Austria, received with acclamations of joy by the Austrian people, and the progress of Hitler through the country received with such scenes of enthusiastic welcome as are unparalleled in history, took the people of this country completely by surprise. They had been carefully educated in the belief that the "independence" of Austria, that is their separation from Germany, was the wish of the Austrian people. The facts that the Austrian Parliament in 1918-19 passed a unanimous vote in favour of union with the Reich, and that Dollfuss, finding that if he held an election the vote would be in favour of the *Anschluss*, had abolished parliament and made himself a dictator, that Schuschnigg his successor had never dared to hold an election, that 40,000 Austrians were in exile across the frontier and thousands in prison without trial, and that Schuschnigg only held power by an armed police with the forces of the allies behind him, made no impression on the people of this country, deceived by a skilful propaganda. Many still believe that Hitler has seized Austria by force of arms against the wishes of the Austrian people. It is a new feature in the history of invasions, for the guns of the invaders to be decorated with wreaths of flowers by the invaded.

In order to get a correct understanding of the real attitude of the great mass of Austrian people, it is necessary to go back to what happened when the war was ended. The quarrel between Austria and Germany which ended in the battle of Sadowa in 1866, was really a quarrel between the two dynasties, the Hohenzollerns and the Habsburgs for supreme power over the German speaking peoples. By the defeat of Austria the Hohenzollerns became supreme, and in 1879 an alliance was formed between the two countries by Bismarck, which led to Germany supporting Austria in her quarrel with Serbia in 1914. During four years Germans of the Reich and Austrian Germans had fought side by side. The long struggle against almost the world whole and the humiliation of defeat which they both suffered welded them together into one people.

On the fall of the Habsburg dynasty, the German Austrians formed a Council of State, and on the 9th of November 1918, this Council of State sent a message to Chancellor Max von Baden of the German Reich:

> "In this hour of great historical crisis the German-Austrian Council of State sends to the German people its fraternal greetings and the warmest wishes for its future. The German-Austrian Council of State expresses the hope that the German people in Austria will have a part in the election of representatives of the Constitutive National Assembly which is to decide the future political order of the German nation."

On November 12th 1918, the Provisional Assembly for German Austria passed the following law:

> "German Austria is a part of the German Republic. Special laws are to regulate the participation of German Austria in the legislation and administration of the German Republic, as well as the extent of the validity of laws and institutions of the German Republic as applied to German Austria."

On November 30th 1918, the Reich government passed the following decree:

> "If the German National Assembly resolves that Austria in accordance with her wish is to be admitted to the German Reich,

then the German-Austrian deputies shall join the Assembly as members with equal rights."

On February 4th 1919, President Dr. Dinghofer addressed the German-Austrian National Assembly as follows:

"Most honourable National Assembly. The day after tomorrow on February 6th, the newly elected Constitutive National Assembly of the German Republic in Weimar meets for the first time. The conditions whereby we participate in the same as rightful members have not yet been reached and indeed not yet created. Nevertheless we cannot ignore this great and significant event. The idea of Greater Germany is not dead for us Germans in these provinces, and never, never was it dead. Like a star glowing out of the darkness the joyous hope of the realization of our longing dream beckons us: in all the sorrow and all the care that now surround us there glows the hope of lasting reunion with our old Motherland. With the greatest enthusiasm we therefore greet our brothers yonder in the Reich. We acclaim them with joy. The German people inseparably united in its entirety, no longer separated by boundary-posts, no longer separated by the jealousy of rulers, shall and must become our homeland again."

In his opening speech at the first session of the German National Assembly at Weimar on February 6th 1919, the people's deputy, Friedrich Ebert, spoke as follows:

"...We also cannot forego the union of the whole German nation in one Reich. Our German Austrian brothers have already declared themselves part of the Greater-German Republic at their National Assembly on November 12th. Now the German Austrian National Assembly has once again amid the greatest enthusiasm sent its greetings and expressed the hope that our

National Assembly and theirs will succeed in re-establishing the link that was broken by force in 1866. German Austria must, they say, be united with the motherland for all time."

At Weimar on 21st February 1919, the following motion was made by the deputies Löbe, Grober, Haase (Berlin), Von Payer, Dr. Count von Posadowsky-Wehner and Dr. Stresemann:

> "May the National Assembly resolve: The National Assembly notes with lively satisfaction the resolutions by which the representatives of German Austria have declared their membership of the German people as a whole. It affirms to its German Austrian brothers that the Germans of the Reich and of Austria constitute an indivisible unit, transcending former state boundaries, and expresses the confident hope that through the negotiations to be entered upon by the governments this inner unity will soon find in settled political forms an expression that will be recognized by all the Powers of the World."

This motion was supported by all parties in the Assembly.

This movement for union between the Germans of Austria and the Germans of the Reich put the three democracies of Great Britain, France and the United States in a somewhat embarrassing position. They had promised self determination to the peoples of Europe, and both Germany and Austria had elected democratic governments and these democratic governments had unanimously decided to unite. On the other hand, the allies had decided that for strategic reasons this union between Germany and Austria must be revented, and an "Independent" Austria created. Accordingly on the 29th of December 1918, the French foreign minister M. Pichon made the following statement:

> "There remains the question of German-Austria. It is serious but it should not alarm us. We have means of solving it so that

THE CASE FOR GERMANY.

it will not bring our enemies the compensations and resources that they hope from it. In settling the new status of Germany and of the ruins of Austria it will be contingent on the Allied Powers to take measures which will decisively reduce the power of Germany to fit proportions and thus deprive her of the chance of indemnifying herself with the Austrian races remaining outside Czecho-Slovakia, Poland and Yugo-Slavia, for what she will irrevocably have lost in any case by sanctioning our victory. This victory must therefore in the first place be transformed into all its just consequences and into the application of the rights which it gives us over the vanquished, to remove the possibility of these again endangering the security and freedom of the world."

Article 80 of the Treaty of Versailles was as follows:

"Germany acknowledges and will respect strictly the independence of Austria, within the frontiers which may be fixed in a treaty between that State and the Principal Allied and Associated Powers; she agrees that this independence shall be inalienable, except with the consent of the Council of the League of Nations",

which meant referring it to the Greek Kalends.

The German delegates signed this clause, but made the following protest:

"In Article 80 is demanded the permanent recognition of Austrian independence within the boundaries laid down by the Peace Treaty of the Allied and Associated Governments with Germany. Germany never has had, and never will have the intention of altering the German-Austrian frontier by force. But should the population of Austria, whose history and culture have been closely linked with its kindred German country for thousands of years, wish to re-establish with Germany the connection that was only dissolved recently by a military decision, then Germany cannot pledge herself to oppose the wish of her German brothers in Austria, since the right of self-determination of peoples must apply generally and not solely to the detriment of Germany. Any other procedure would be in contradiction to the principles laid down in the Congress speech of President Wilson on February 11th, 1918."

In drawing up the constitution of the German Reich, another attempt was made to keep the door open for union with Austria. The following two clauses were introduced:

> Article 2. "The territory of the Reich consists of the territories of the German countries. Other territories can be admitted to the Reich by law if their population desires it in accordance with the right of self-determination."
>
> Article 61, par. 2. "After union with the German Reich, German Austria shall receive the right of participating in the Reich Council with the number of votes corresponding with her population. Until such time the representatives of German Austria shall have an advisory vote."

On September 2nd 1919, the following note was sent by President Clemenceau to the President of the German Reich.

> "The Allied and Associated Powers have taken note of the German constitution of August 11th 1919. They confirm that the conditions of Paragraph 2 of Article 61 constitute a formal violation of Article 80 of the Peace Treaty signed at Versailles on June 28th, 1919.
> It is a double violation:
> **1.** Article 61, in stipulating the admission of Austria to the *Reichsrat*, likens this Republic to the German provinces which

constitute the German Empire; this is incompatible with the observance of Austria's independence.

2. In allowing and regulating the participation of Austria in the *Reichsrat*, Article 61 creates a political bond and a common political action between Germany and Austria, in complete contradiction to the independence of the latter.

The Allied and Associated Powers therefore, having reminded the German Government that Article 178 of the German Constitution declares that the 'conditions of the Treaty of Versailles cannot be affected by the constitution', summon the German Government to take the proper steps to annul this violation forthwith, by declaring Article 61, paragraph 2, void.

With the reservation as to further measures in the event of refusal, and indeed on the basis of the Treaty (namely, Article 429), the Allied and Associated Powers inform the German Government that this violation of its obligations in an essential point will oblige the Powers to extend their occupation immediately on the right bank of the Rhine, if their just demand be not complied with within 14 days of the date of this note."

The clause was withdrawn.

Since then the agitation for the *Anschluss* has never ceased, and has grown in intensity as Germany under Hitler once more became a free nation.

After the abortive rising and the deplorable assassination of Dollfuss, the movement in favour of the *Anschluss* was savagely suppressed.

Staying in Salzburg at the time, we saw young peasants from the hills being marched in as prisoners. The Castle was full of prisoners and several were shot without trial although they had not been near Vienna and could have had nothing to do with the assassination.

When Schuschnigg broke all his promises to Hitler, and announced his travesty of a plebiscite, the Austrian pot boiled over. There was no register of voters, no arrangements to protect the secrecy of the ballot, and only one voting card with "Independent Austria, Heil Schuschnigg, Ja" printed on it. Anyone wishing to vote No, had to cut out a card of the same size, write on it No and hand it openly to Schuschnigg officials who were the only people allowed at the polling stations, with the probability of arrest and imprisonment.

On the 11th of March the following telegram was sent by Dr. Seyss-Inquart to Hitler:

> "The provisional Government of Austria which, after the resignation of the Schuschnigg government, consider it their duty to restore calm and order in Austria, direct to the German Government the urgent request to support them in their duty and to help them in preventing bloodshed. To this end they ask the German Government to send German troops as soon as possible."

After the receipt of this telegram, German troops marched in and the *Anschluss* was accomplished without the loss of a single life.

The Sudeten Germans

At the time when I am finishing this book, the governments of Europe have solved the vexed problems of the Sudeten Germans, and the Hungarians forcibly included in Czecho-Slovakia - another inheritance from the peace treaties.

Czecho-Slovakia contains Germans, Slovaks, Hungarians, Poles, Rumanians, Ruthenians and Czechs, and over all these alien people bundled together by the framers of the peace treaties into one nation, the Czechs have a small majority which has enabled them under the outward form of democracy to keep supreme power in their own hands. Lord Balfour declared when the State of Czecho-Slovakia was brought into existence, that these new European States were built up on the

THE CASE FOR GERMANY.

principle of little nations on the victorious side seizing the territories of a country that was defeated, and holding them on a cut-throat basis which cannot be defended. None of these various races love one another, but all are agreed on a hatred of Czech domination, and both the Germans and the Slovaks have petitioned the League for freedom and independence.

There can be no question that the Sudeten Germans have suffered cruelly under Czech rule. The glass industry has been allowed to fall into decay, they are denied equality of political rights, they have great difficulty in getting employment, and a large number are slowly dying of starvation. The statistics as to disease from malnutrition among the German children are appalling. Until recently thousands have been imprisoned without trial.

Their terrible condition has naturally excited the greatest indignation among their German brothers in the Reich, and Hitler's task has been to prevent any rash act on either side of the frontier which might lead to war.

The reason why all Europe was so interested in Czecho-Slovakia is because Bohemia, now part of Czecho-Slovakia, surrounded by mountains, is the natural citadel of central Europe. It is for this reason that the treaty between the Czechs and the Soviet was so dangerous. If Bohemia were in possession of the Soviet army, they could accomplish that Asiatic conquest of Europe which has so nearly happened more than once in the past. The treaty has now been denounced and the door for an inroad into Europe of Asiatic hordes under the flag of the hammer and the sickle, bolted and barred.

When the Sudeten German question came to a head, and the pot long simmering boiled over, Hitler had to deal with a very complex situation. The German people were difficult to restrain, the Sudeten Germans were in rebellion and the Communist party in Czecho-Slovakia hoped to use the trouble to promote a European war, while it was impossible to trust Benes who had made so many promises he had never kept in the past.

While a party in Czecho-Slovakia wished to provoke an armed intervention by France, Hitler was doing his best to avoid the necessity. He had only to send an armed force from Austria into Slovakia, and promise independence to all the minorities and home rule to the Slovaks, for Czecho-Slovakia to fall to pieces, a result which the Communists were prepared to face if only France could be persuaded to intervene, - an intervention which Hitler had to do everything he could to prevent.

The Runciman report in favour of the cession of the Sudeten German area to Germany without delay, cleared the air, and when Hitler proposed this solution to Chamberlain at their first meeting, Chamberlain was able to persuade his Cabinet, Daladier and Benes to accept this solution.

Between Chamberlain's first and second visit to see Hitler, certain incidents had taken place in Czecho-Slovakia which were not reported by our Press, but were witnessed by a friend of mine who was on the spot at the time. My friend entered Prague on September 20th, and found the Czechs very depressed at the thought of giving up the Sudeten German territory. That evening a wireless message was sent out by the Prague station, that Churchill had overthrown Chamberlain, become Prime Minister, and flown to Paris to arrange for war with Germany. Next day Prague was seething with excitement, and bills were posted in the town comparing the military strength of Germany with the military strength of Great Britain, France, the USSR. and the USA: The Prime Minister resigned and M. Hodza became Prime Minister.

In the meantime my friend had motored on to Eger. He arrived on the Wednesday afternoon, and found that the handing over of the Sudeten German area having been agreed to, the Czech government had allowed the Germans to take over the management of the town which was decorated everywhere with the German flag, and the people rejoicing in the streets. The Czech police were arranging to leave the town in the most peaceable manner.

On the Thursday morning M. Hodza became Prime Minister, and on the Thursday afternoon, a telegram was received from the new government that the Czechs were again going to take over the town. There was a hasty hiding away of flags and decorations, and in the evening the Czech troops marched into a silent town with deserted streets, everyone hiding behind closed doors.

My friend motored on the frontier, and found bridges being blown up and machine gun emplacements being erected. It was evident that Benes had made up his mind for one last gamble for war, and that the message sent out by the new government that they adhered to the handing over of the Sudeten German area, was merely intended to put off time.

All these facts were of course known to Hitler, and caused him to draw up his ultimatum for immediate entry.

His proposal that Czech troops should retire and the German troops advance into the area was the only plan to prevent bloodshed between the Czech and German population. Runciman had already stated that it was necessary to act quickly to prevent civil war, and it is difficult to understand why Chamberlain rejected a plan which was unanimously adopted by the four powers a week later.

The ultimatum drawn up by Hitler might have been written in a more conciliatory manner, but the map accompanying it agreed closely with the map already prepared, and with the territory ultimately given up, and no difficulty was found in adhering to the time table he had originally drawn up. The flight of some of the Czechs from the Sudeten German area was quite unnecessary, as was proved by the quiet occupation of the area by the German troops without any disturbance of the existing population. The fact is that the Continental peasant from long and bitter experience over many centuries, whenever he hears of the approach of an army packs up his household goods and bolts.

During the interview with Chamberlain, Hitler for the first time threatened to use force and enter the Sudeten area even though opposed by Czech troops if it was not ceded at once. It seems to me inconceivable that we would have plunged Europe into war because Hitler insisted on an immediate occupation of territory which had already been ceded to him, millions of lives being sacrificed over a dispute about a time table.

Hitler had pledged himself in his speech on March 7th 1936, that all adjustments of territory between Germany and other nations should be made by agreement and has carried out his pledge, though he seemed to come near to breaking it. It is probable that at the last moment Benes would have yielded as he could only trust the Czechs in his army, the whole Sudeten German population would have risen behind his troops, and Czecho-Slovakia would have fallen to pieces though no German soldier had advanced beyond the Sudeten German area. It is significant of the condition to which the German population had been reduced, that Hitler said that on his entry he had seen for the first time people weeping for joy and that the first thing the German troops had to do was to bring in large quantities of bread for the starving people.

Extract from a Czech Schoolbook

"Who loves the Czechs - Hail to him! Long life to him!"
"Who loves the Russians - Hail to him! Long life to him!"
"Who loves the Serbs - Hail to him! Long life to him!"
"Who loves the Slovenes - Hail to him! Long life to him!"
"Who loves the Hungarians - Strike him down!"
"Who loves the Germans - Strike him down!"

11

Acts of "Aggression" by Germany

In order to get a true perspective towards what has taken place in Central Europe during the last five years, it is necessary to grasp the fact that what we have been witnessing is a rebellion of the German peoples in Central Europe against the peace treaties.

Hitler has been the leader, and the Nazi movement the spear head, but the rebellion was not confined to Germany, but included the German population of Austria and the Sudeten German area.

The allies had made an "Independent" state of Austria in spite of the unanimous vote of the first Austrian parliament for union with the Reich, and had handed over the Sudeten Germans to the Czechs in spite of their protests, for purely strategic reasons.

Dollfuss in order to maintain Austria as an independent state had to abolish the Austrian parliament, and rule as an absolute dictator, and Schuschnigg had to continue this policy. The Nazi movement progressed at first more rapidly in Austria than in Germany.

Once we have grasped the central fact that we have been witnessing a rebellion of the German peoples, all that has happened in the last five years falls into place and becomes intelligible.

Having risen in rebellion against the articles in the peace treaties which applied to them, they have re-armed, have occupied with troops their own frontiers, and have taken over the administration of their own rivers, railways and canals. In addition the German people of

Austria have joined with the German people of the Reich under one government.

All these acts have taken place within territory inhabited by and belonging to the German people, and have in no way interfered with the rights of any other nation. In addition, with the consent of the three powers and of the government of Czecho-Slovakia, the Sudeten German area has been joined to the Reich. This addition to German territory was advised by our commissioner Lord Runciman, and has been described by Sir John Simon as an act of justice. We are told by the enemies of Germany in this country that these acts of the German people were aggressive, violent and illegal acts, and we must proceed to examine these three accusations.

An act of aggression involves interference with other nations. It is not regarded by us as an aggressive act on our part to spend vast sums on munitions, or if we chose to do so to introduce conscription. If the Union between England and Scotland was taking place to-day, it could not be described by other nations as an act of aggression on our part. As all these re-adjustments made by German peoples took place in territory which contained an almost totally German population, we must give a verdict of not guilty when they are accused of acts of aggression.

The second accusation is that the German people have acted in a violent manner. As all these changes have been accomplished in a perfectly orderly way amid the rejoicing consent of the populations concerned, and without the loss of a single life, the charge of violence falls to the ground. There are people in this country who talk of the "invasion" of Austria. An "invasion" in which the people of the "invaded" country decorate the guns of the "invader" is something new in history.

The third accusation of having acted in an illegal manner is made under two heads. They are accused of breaking international law by tearing up the Treaty of Versailles, and also of acting against the protests of the League of Nations.

Let us begin by examining the first accusation. It has long been the custom among civilized nations who have been at war, after an

THE CASE FOR GERMANY.

armistice has been declared, for the delegates of both nations to meet in conference and draw up a treaty together. Such a treaty is regarded as binding on both parties until owing to changing circumstances one party or the other denounces the treaty and a new treaty is drawn up. It has also always been understood that no act of war takes place after the armistice has been signed.

The allies when engaged in drawing up the Treaty of Versailles, departed from both these customs which have been recognised by all civilized nations. **The Treaty of Versailles was drawn up by the allies without the German delegates being admitted.** They were then called in and graciously allowed to suggest certain modifications which were promptly rejected, and told to sign. They signed under protest, and said that the German people would never regard the treaty as binding. **The second departure from civilized practice was the continuance after the armistice had been signed of the blockade which was starving the German people.** The signature of the German delegates was made the condition for raising the blockade.

A treaty between two nations is of the nature of a contract between two men, and both parties are expected to carry it out. But if one of the parties after signing the contract can convince the judge that he signed it by compulsion with a pistol held to his head, no court would uphold the contract.

In the case of the entry into the neutral zone of the German troops, there is a plausible case against Germany. **Her defence is that France, by making a treaty with the Soviet directed against Germany, had already torn up the Treaty of Locarno,** and was fully warned of the view that would be taken of this act in Germany. Even if the verdict goes against Germany, and she did commit an illegal act, the crime of occupying your own territory with your own troops cannot be regarded as a very serious one.

The other accusation is that Germany acted in an illegal manner in defying the protests of the League of Nations. The victorious powers decided to set up a perpetual committee which they invited other nations to join, and which they called the League of Nations. Germany was excluded at the beginning and the USA. washed their hands of the whole affair. The main object of the League was to keep the peace treaties inviolate, but it also took on other international duties. Those joining it signed a covenant promising not to make war on each other, but to refer matters of dispute to the League, and in certain articles the League took power to use force through its members against any nation which it had named as an aggressor.

The League arrogated to itself a legal status which would not be recognised in international law. It had no more authority over other nations than any other alliance of the powers. The members of the League were of course bound by the terms of their contract while they remained members but if they chose to leave the League, the League had no jurisdiction over them and protests passed by the League had no more legal status than if they had been passed by a Mothers Meeting.

International law has grown up slowly through certain customs being finally accepted by all nations, and it is possible that if a League of Nations had been formed at some time before the war when the whole world was at peace, and had in the first instance been a voluntary body with no compulsory powers, it might in time have been recognised by all nations that its decisions were binding; but a League set up by the victors after a war to enforce the maintenance of a status quo which was intolerable to the conquered nations, was doomed to failure. We must therefore return a verdict of not guilty under the second accusation of illegal action.

The German peoples have only claimed and taken such rights as are granted to all nations, and have carried out their programme among themselves and within their own territory with the exception of the union of the Sudeten German area to the Reich which was done with the consent of the other three powers. Such action is neither aggressive, violent nor illegal, and in no way injures the interests of external powers.

Another accusation made against Germany that she uses the threat of force while the League and the Democracies confine themselves to

THE CASE FOR GERMANY.

sweet reasonableness and would never use a potential force to get their own way. **They blame Hitler for having re-armed Germany. Surely that is an absurd accusation when France at the time he re-armed had an army of five hundred thousand men on a peace footing, and the Soviet an army of one million three hundred thousand men.**

Hitler has only once threatened to use force, when he stated that after a certain date he would if necessary force his way into the territory already assigned to him.

The fact is that in the present crude and barbaric conditions of the relations between nations, every nation has to be "well heeled" before going into a conference.

The allies used potential force to compel the Germans to sign the Treaty of Versailles and to prevent the union of Austria with Germany, and the League refused all concessions to Germany, and ignored the appeals of minorities in Czecho-Slovakia, because behind the League was the army of France.

It is now generally agreed that the Versailles Treaty was most unjust to Germany, but if Germany had not defied the League and begun to re-arm, she would to-day be in the position she was in 1932. Concessions are not made by one nation to another nation because they are just, but because it is dangerous to refuse.

It is true that Chamberlain agreed to the cession of the Sudeten German area because he thought it was just and right, and there are instances in our history when we have acted even to our own detriment on the merits of a case; but I know of no instance of such an action by any other nation except ourselves.

The whole conception of the League as a super state was built on a foundation of force, and the complaint of the parties of the Left in this country is not that the League was built on a foundation of force, but that when the time for action came the whole machine broke down, the various members of the League refusing to fight. In reply to a statement that we had forty nations behind us over the Abyssinian question, Chamberlain said, "Yes, they are behind us but not by our side".

It is only fair to say that the Opposition claim that the mere threat by the League would be sufficient if it was properly organised for military action; but there always is the danger that the other side will call your bluff. A revolver charged with blank cartridges is a dangerous weapon when going into a quarrel.

We are re-arming to-day not because Great Britain or the Empire is in the slightest danger from attack, but because we want to go into any discussion with any other power as "well heeled" as they are.

When Hitler says "the army is Germany", has not that lesson been taught him by all that has happened since the Armistice was signed? If after the signing of the Armistice the army of Germany though in retreat had still been in being, the Treaty of Versailles would have been a very different document. Would France have entered the Ruhr if there had been the German army to oppose her? **An unarmed nation will get no justice from the other nations.**

Hitler says "the army is Germany". Is it not equally true that our navy is the British Empire? We have built the Empire by force, we hold it by force, and we will defend it by force, and we possess it intact to-day because our navy is far stronger than the navy of any other Power.

"Ah", my critic will reply, "the League, the Allies, France and Great Britain only use force in a just and righteous cause. All other nations and more especially Germany and Italy use it in an unrighteous cause", which reminds me of a story told me by my father. When he was a boy Scotland was under the tyranny of a rigid Sabbatarianism. One day he was scolded for having laughed on the Sabbath day. He retorted that he had heard the minister laugh on the Sabbath. "Ah", was the reply, "but that was a Holy smile".

12

The Dance of Death

We have recently developed a habit of holding public meetings to denounce the sins of our neighbours. On such occasions violent and exaggerated statements are made and the whole audience worked up to a condition of glorious indignation and intense moral satisfaction with themselves thanking God as the Pharisee in the Temple, that they are not as this Publican. I cannot find in the scriptures that Our Lord tells us to meet together to confess the sins of our brothers, instead of confessing our own sins, and we are especially warned not to pass judgment. We, like the village gossip, always assume the worst. What effect are such meetings likely to have in the countries which are denounced? We have recently had some experience owing to the German press having at last taken to hitting back, digging out some black passages in our past history, and describing them with the gross exaggeration customary in political propaganda. These attacks in the German press have produced a feeling of intense indignation here. We may criticise our own sins, but are not going to have any damned foreigner doing it for us. It is none of his business, we say. Curiously enough the Germans have just the same feeling about things we say about them, and so the piling up of ill feeling is growing on both sides every day.

It is generally admitted by serious students to-day that the war of 1914 had no legitimate cause, if any cause for war can be regarded as legitimate. There have been in the past economic wars, dynastic wars, religious wars and wars for the conquest of territory, but in 1914 the nations of Europe had no quarrel with each other, and the whole world was prospering and increasing in trade.

It is true that we were very jealous of the rapid increase of the German export trade, and suspicious of the Fleet they were building although it was much less than half the size of our own, but I doubt if any merchant feeling the pinch of German competition in the world market would have regarded that competition as a justifiable reason for war.

The quarrel between Austria and Serbia could have been settled by reasonable negotiation between Austria and Russia without disturbing the rest of Europe. The only outcome of the war has been that millions of lives were thrown away, and a distracted Europe and an impoverished world left as the only tangible result.

Looking back on those years before the war, I realise that an insidious propaganda against Germany had been carried on for a long time, - why or by whom or with what intent I do not know, - which was gradually poisoning our minds. It is true Germany had the most powerful land army in the world, that the German Emperor had the gift of saying boastful and irritating things, and that there was a pan-German society which amused itself by drawing imaginary maps of a German European Empire. There had also been some trouble over the Agadir incident, when the German Emperor woke up to find that we had presented France with the whole of Morocco which did not belong to us; but there was no justification for saying that Germany meditated wars of conquest, and as an actual fact the German foreign office was in dread of the power of Russia.

What were the facts? Since the war of 1870, for which France and Germany were equally to blame, up to 1914 Germany had been at peace with all the world. We on the other hand had been constantly at war. We had invaded and conquered Egypt, we had made war on the Boers, we had fought in Africa and on the frontiers of India, and had annexed Burma. The gates of the temple of Janus had never been closed; yet we were firmly convinced that we were a peaceful non-aggressive people, and Germany an aggressive military nation.

Now that no serious student of the events leading up to 1914 [can still claim] that the German government was to blame any more than any other European government including our own, this legend about an aggressive Germany is obviously false; yet it is still believed by many people in this country, and we are told that Hitler is the successor of the Kaiser, and aims at the military conquest of Europe. The last war was psychological, it had no basis on realities, and if there is another war in Europe it will also be psychological.

In the old days of mercenary armies in Europe, two kings might quarrel and let loose their armies on each other without troubling to consult the people, whose first knowledge that war had been declared was when soldiers of both sides began looting their farms. To-day, now that we have conscript armies, it is necessary for the government before it can declare war to rouse the peoples of two countries to such a hatred of each other, that decent Englishmen and decent Germans get out their rifles and try to kill each other. This is done by means of propaganda.

There are of course powerful interests in every country to whom war means big profits and who may be secretly engaged in financing propaganda and, as I have shown elsewhere, the Socialists and Communists in Europe to-day are exerting every effort to set the four western powers at war; but this is not sufficient to explain the rapid spread of an infection over a country producing all the symptoms of mental rabies. The Press have no scruples about stimulating this mental intoxication if it sells a few more copies of the paper, and do not hesitate about publishing shocking lies, and using the poster to excite the public.

The most serious danger to Peace is the utter want of any feeling of responsibility on the part of the British, French and American Press and wireless. Let me take a recent example. The annexation of Bohemia and Moravia by the German government, and the joining of Memel to the Reich, has caused considerable excitement in this country. It is therefore a time when those responsible for news should do their best to calm and not excite public imagination. The B.B.C. sent out a message that the German government had told the Lithuanian government that if they did not hand over Memel, German planes would bomb the capital of Lithuania, and that while the Lithuanian parliament was meeting, German bombing planes flew backwards and forwards overhead.

There are poisons known to medicine which are called cumulative poisons. One drop will do no harm, but it remains in the body waiting for the next drop and the next and the next, until sufficient of the poison has accumulated to produce illness and death. The same is true of poisons to the mind. We read in the Press a lie about Germany, next day we read part of a speech denouncing Germany, on the Sunday we hear a sermon in which Germany is attacked. We pick up a magazine lying on the club table and there is an article abusing Germany. And so day by day and week by week and month by month this cumulative poison collects in our minds until the day comes when it produces a mental fever in which all sense of proportion is lost and we are controlled by the horrible delusion that it is our duty to go out and kill.

An interesting example of this occurred in the House of Commons the other day. The leader of the Labour party and the leader of the Liberal party both accused Franco of having dropped from his planes chocolate boxes containing infernal machines to blow children to pieces. There is a well known morbid disease known as persecution mania which often results in the sufferer committing murder. Both these men have reached this dangerous mental condition. They will not have to commit the murder themselves, but will send other men out to kill and to be killed.

When once war has been declared, the governments of both sides take charge of the propaganda machine and pour out lies about the people on the other side in order to keep hatred at a killing point. Many will remember that during the first year of the war, it was decided by both sides on the French front to have a truce at Christmas with the result that the German and English soldiers got so friendly that if the higher command had not stopped it at once, they would have refused

THE CASE FOR GERMANY.

to go on killing each other. I remember the first time I visited France during the war. I went to the camouflage factory and was astounded to find that our officers liked the Germans and only began to use bad language when the Portuguese were mentioned. The hatred of the German which was felt in Great Britain did not extend to the fighting line. As I watched Chinese labourers, French peasant girls, German prisoners and English soldiers all working happily together I wondered what we were fighting about.

It is also necessary, in order to keep the war fever at its height, **to invent a slogan. Our slogan was that we were fighting to save democracy,** - the victory of the allies having resulted in the abolition of parliament and the setting up of dictators in nearly every country in Europe.

I have during my life seen the nations of Europe hurled at each other's throats in a meaningless slaughter by means of lying propaganda, and when I see the same thing going on to-day in an aggravated form, I confess I am very much afraid. The German people who have been carrying through a revolution against enormous odds, have doubtless done many things of which we cannot approve, but these things have not only been exaggerated out of all proportion, but have been successfully used to rouse the most dangerous and bloodthirsty of all human emotions, - moral indignation, and the church has been pressed into service in order to bring us nearer to war. Everywhere the gospel of hate is being preached in the Press and from the pulpit. **We are told by those preaching this gospel that they have no hostility to the German people but only to the German government, the wicked Hitler and the dreadful Nazis.** If that is true, surely the right way to go about it is to persuade the German people that our view and not their view is right. Surely a hatred of Hitler is not a reason for killing millions of Germans, and incidentally killing millions of Englishmen in the process. If war is declared against Germany, every German whatever his private opinions will line up behind Hitler to defend his fatherland, and after a furious and bloody war, nothing will have been settled and Europe ruined.

We are told that Hitler is going to do this and is going to do that; let us at any rate wait and see if he does do any of these things before we dream of plunging into war.

The danger of the situation in this country is that good well-meaning people have got trapped by this propaganda and are beginning to think that the killing of Germans is a righteous and Christian act. If these people would go to Germany and visit some of the little German towns and wander about among the decent kindly people and say to themselves when they see a German workman returning to his home, *"I am going to kill that man"*, and a German mother sitting in a public garden with her children, *"I am going to make her a widow, and I am going to drop bombs upon this town and set it blazing in flames with the tortured people dying in agony in the ruins"*, all this in the name of the Christian religion, I believe they would go away shuddering at committing such devilry in the name of Christ.

When savage tribes wish to make war upon another tribe, they work their young men up to the killing point by means of war dances which produce the necessary mental intoxication. Our method to-day is more elaborate, but the object and the outcome is the same. The dance of death is getting wilder and wilder in this country, until nothing will satisfy us except a holocaust of blood. It is obvious that the war propaganda in this country, and in America, cannot be kept going without a large expenditure, and the investment of capital in buying up politicians, managing governments, and controlling the British and American Press. It is impossible to find out who really owns the big British dailies behind the scenes, but it is evident that most of them dare not publish anything but anti-German news. Probably the only really free press in England today, are the local weekly newspapers.

Those who handle large sums of money are the International financiers, who do not spend money for ideological reasons, but only to make more money. It was not till I read the story of the political activities of the great Jewish banking firm Kuhn Loeb and Co, and the way in which they controlled American Presidents, and financed the Japanese

THE CASE FOR GERMANY.

war against Russia, that I realised the connection between war and high finance, which is the polite name for money lending on a big scale.

We cannot imagine our dear old orthodox British banks indulging in such unorthodox practices, but they pick up the crumbs which fall from the masters table. The profits are made in handling big loans, the general public finally holding the baby. Since the war, by means of propaganda, the American public have been persuaded to invest large sums in loans to bankrupt South American States, every penny of which has been lost, the financiers making their profit and clearing out. We had a ramp in the cotton industry, organised by the "City", which robbed the Lancashire workers of their savings and ruined the industry.

The richest field for plunder for the international financier is war and rumours of war. Owing to the present bad temper among European nations, some five thousand millions, if we include the U.S.A., is being spent on armaments, with no control on profits here or in America, and most of the money is being borrowed, while war means the borrowing of huge sums by the government at high rates of interest. It is obvious then, that while war ruins nations, it is the best way in which high finance can make enormous profits, the burden of interest being borne by future tax payers.

In the second place, as long as Germany and Italy are under their present governments, they will not touch foreign loans, and Germany by her method of internal economy and trading has eliminated the international financier, and those who make profits by playing with foreign exchanges. That is doubtless why the government is being forced by the "City" to start a trade war with Germany. If the economic methods devised by Germany are successful, and spread to other nations, and if Hitler succeeds in his policy of establishing permanent peace in Europe, the high financier will cease to be able to exist. It is therefore their main interest today to plunge the four powers into war, in order to destroy Germany and Italy. Having failed in September to start Europe fighting over a time table, they are now trying to bring in the U.S.A., which has already begun a trade war against Germany. It would be interesting to know the real origin of Roosevelt's outburst about defending *"Christianity, democracy and international good faith"*. Who pulled the strings and sat grinning in his bank parlour in New York?

The organisation of mass propaganda here and in the U.S.A., by financial groups, means the end of democracy, which is based on the free expression of opinion and putting both sides before the people. Not only is the Press and the B.B.C. controlled, but the House of Commons itself is being intimidated, as the Members of Parliament fear their constituents whose minds have been poisoned by mass propaganda. There are many Members of Parliament opposed to our hostility to Germany, but they are afraid to speak in the House. In fact, we have reached the extraordinary position in this "free and democratic" country, that the only place where a fearless discussion is possible and takes place, is in the House of Lords, where the members, separated by their exalted position from the tyranny of machine-made democratic opinion, can speak freely what they believe, and excellent speeches are made opposing our hostility to Germany.

Freedom of speech, a high level of intelligence, and a genuine desire for the public good, apart from the low motives of political life, has deserted the House of Commons, and taken refuge in the House of Lords.

Once their propaganda has been successful, the governments of democratic countries have to yield as our Government has yielded to the outcry about the annexation of Bohemia and Moravia. Only Hitler and Mussolini are strong enough to say No and will keep the peace unless we and France compel them to draw the sword. Unfortunately in this country the "City" pulls the strings, and while our young men will be fighting and dying under the delusion that they were defending Christianity and democracy, they would really be fighting to make profits for the international financiers.

The vultures of finance gorge on war and rumours of war, and millions of lives are sacrificed to fill their money chests.

13

Our Future Policy Towards Germany

The Peace Pact having been signed with Germany, and the German people in Central Europe having accomplished their union under one Reich, with the exception of one minor area, Danzig, the question before the people of this country is what is to be our policy towards Germany in the future.

We must agree that it has not been a wise policy in the past. While on the one hand admitting that the conditions forced on them by the Treaty of Versailles were unfair and would have to be revised, on the other hand instead of arranging with them that the revisal be done by agreement, we have protested against every step they took in this direction. Why could we not have done what we did in the case of Turkey in agreeing to the fortification of the Dardanelles? - a matter much more vital to us than anything happening in Central Europe. Either we could have adopted the policy of the Opposition, said No, and been prepared to back our No with war if necessary, or we could have agreed to the revisal by mutual consent.

Mr. Chamberlain, in arranging for a conference of the four Powers to settle the Sudeten German problem, has adopted the policy which we should have adopted from the beginning. The Sudeten German question differed from anything that had happened before, as up to that time Germany had been engaged in internal re-organization and in completing, by the union with Austria, the policy begun by Bismarck, - a policy which was entirely their own affair. The problem of Sudeten Germany was the first to involve the interests of another state, and was further complicated by the alliance between Czecho-Slovakia and France. Germany was therefore quite right in accepting the offer to settle the matter by agreement according to the promise made by Hitler in his speech of March 7th 1936.

Mr. Chamberlain having initiated this new policy of consultation among the four Powers on any point of disagreement, it is all the more necessary to define our attitude towards Germany.

In order to be able to do this, we must begin by considering what are the vital necessities of the German people, and whether there is any reason why we should oppose them. In considering this question we must put on one side our democratic sentiments, and our disapproval of some of the things the German Government have done within their own country, and look into the question on a purely business basis from the point of view of our Imperial interests.

To deal first with the needs of the German people. There are 80 million Germans living on a small area in Europe with a comparatively poor soil, who cannot like the French obtain all the food they want from the fertile soil of their own country. It is therefore evident that they must either be satisfied with a very low standard of comfort and an underfed population, or develop external trade, or undertake military conquest of new territory.

In spite of the alarm of the Opposition, we may dismiss the idea that Germany is meditating ventures of military conquest. Such a policy must result in ruin and disaster, and though partly successful would not improve her economic position. Even if Hitler is the military filibuster which the Opposition foolishly imagine him to be, we may take it for granted that the average German citizen would rather trade than fight. The days of military conquest and subjugation of other nations in Europe are over, as there is no genuine economic advantage to be

THE CASE FOR GERMANY.

obtained from it. This is clearly perceived by the German people and in course of time will doubtless be understood by our own politicians who in this matter are mentally behind the times.

The only alternative therefore is extended trade, and Germany is making every effort she can to carry out this policy. While trading with any and every nation, she has looked round the world to see whether there is any region open to her which is economically undeveloped and which would supply her with the raw materials she requires. Putting on one side for a time her claim for colonies, and realising the importance of doing nothing to arouse the jealousy and suspicion of Great Britain, she has agreed to a strict limitation of her fleet, and is looking for a development of trade on land areas.

If we look at the map of Europe, we shall recognise that the obvious direction for her trade expansion is in the countries situated on the Danube and beyond that the Balkans and Turkey, along the lines of the old overland trade route from Asia to Europe. She has already developed a considerable trade with the states on the Danube and with the Balkan states, and is projecting a great canal taking ships up to 1500 tons to connect the Rhine with the Danube.

There can be no question that there are great possibilities of development in these economically backward countries, and that Germany will be of the greatest assistance to them, enabling them to take advantage of modern scientific methods of production.

Although she has been compelled by her economic position to enter into special trade agreements, she is not attempting to claim any monopoly and if she is successful in developing these countries economically, we shall reap some of the benefits. Surely with our world trade and vast Empire, we can allow Germany to cultivate this garden lying at her door. Doubtless these countries will be included in the German "sphere of influence", whatever that may mean. I cannot see that this is any business of ours, as no vital interests of the British Empire can be affected by the development of trade in the central parts of Europe. It is the right of every nation to adopt the form of government they prefer, and we have no more right to try and compel nations to adopt our political theories by acts of war than the Roman Catholic Church has the right to crush Protestantism by promoting war in Europe. We are a business people engaged in world trade and, avoiding all ideologies, we must look at the whole question from a purely business point of view. To repeat the famous phrase of Bismarck with a difference. - The whole of the Balkans is not worth the life of one British soldier. Surely possessing the world and the fatness thereof, we need not grudge her this line of development.

There are rumours that the Soviet is breaking up and that the next great national movement is going to be in the Ukraine which formed an independent republic after the war and was afterwards massacred into submission by the Soviet. The Ukrainians in Poland who have been badly treated by the Poles are demanding Home Rule, and the Ukrainians in Czecho-Slovakia are evidently in a restless condition. The Ukraine includes the black soil wheat area of Russia on the Dneiper, and could supply unlimited wheat to Germany in return for manufactured goods and will naturally enter into close relations with Germany who will be her natural protectors against the Soviet. Therefore if once an independent Ukraine republic was established and entered into friendly relations with Germany, we should be glad that the essential needs of Germany for raw materials had been satisfied. To quote Hitler, "A nation which is satisfied and well-fed is more likely to keep the peace than a nation which is dissatisfied and hungry."

Ah, our Opposition will reply, but Germany will be exercising throughout all these regions that vague and mysterious thing called a sphere of influence. As long as they are exercising a sphere of influence [that] results in these nations being contented and well supplied with goods, and therefore secures the peace of Europe, why should we object, and oppose these natural developments which are inevitable because they are based upon the facts of geography. The answer is there is no alternative plan except to make war on the German people and reduce them to such desperate impoverishment and slaughter of so many of their youth, that they are again brought to their condition after the Thirty Years War and will require a century to recover. Mr. Lloyd George says we can crush them like an eggshell. He would find the eggshell made of tempered steel.

I have searched the pages of Hansard containing the speeches of the Opposition in the recent debate on a vote of censure against the Government's foreign policy, with a view to finding out what is their alternative policy to the one advocated by Mr. Chamberlain. This alternative policy was given by Mr. Dalton and is worthy of quotation in full.

> "There is once more a possibility, it may not last much longer. There is still one more chance for British diplomacy to bring together into an effective combination all those nations in the East of Europe who are threatened by this German push to the East. They are still there a potential combination, the Soviet Union, Poland, Rumania, Yugo-Slavia, Turkey and Greece. They are all members of the League of Nations, to which we and France still belong. You have still there a potential formidable force if it could be welded together for peace and for organised resistance to further endeavours to dislocate Europe."

It is unfortunate that men in the responsible position of leaders of the Labour party should be so ignorant of the real situation in Europe to-day. Germany far from dislocating Europe is consolidating Europe by helping to adjust the injustices caused by the peace treaties, and has no intention of threatening any of these countries with aggression. France who has signed a peace pact with Germany and is anxious to develop her trade relations with her, would not support the Labour policy, and the Soviet is too busy with internal affairs and with Japan, to indulge in the venture of a European war at the call of our Labour party. When Mr. Dalton's delegate called on the governments of Poland, Rumania,

Yugo-Slavia, Turkey and Greece, they would receive his proposals with astonishment, and tell him that they were much too busy making profitable trade agreements with Germany.

Mr. Dalton had great hopes of the new Prime Minister of Hungary. If he had listened over the wireless the other day he would have heard the Prime Minister saying that the closest bonds of friendship united Hungary to Germany and Italy, because they would be for ever grateful to them for enabling them to recover their stolen territories from Czecho-Slovakia.

Our policy in Europe in the past has been called securing "the balance of power" which meant that if ever we thought one nation in Europe was getting more powerful than the other nations we made it our business to promote war against that nation, and to support war when it came with our money bags, our fleet and expeditionary forces. This policy is openly advocated by Mr. Ramsay Muir who glories in the days of Marlborough and Wellington, and wishes to see them come back again. There can be no question that this policy of the past has cost Europe millions of lives on a hundred battlefields. We not only promoted wars but when war had once begun supported its continuance with our money bags until the war, to quote Mr. Lloyd George, was "fought to a finish", with the result that it ended probably in an unjust treaty which opened the door to future wars.

Can anyone doubt now that if we had adopted Lord Lansdowne's policy in 1917, and made peace with Germany then, we should have saved all the dangers and difficulties of the last twenty years.

To my mind the policy of the Balance of Power is a damnable policy. We have been in the past the evil genius of Europe. It is surely evident that if the policy of the Opposition was adopted, and could be successfully carried out, blocking Germany's natural trade expansion in the Danube basin and in the Balkans, the German people confined to a limited area with no hope of commercial development, would be compelled to fight in order to live. The choice therefore is between Mr. Chamberlain's policy of allowing Germany a free area for commercial expansion, or war - a war in which Germany would be fighting for her life.

The maddest of all nightmares from which the Opposition suffer, is that Germany would attempt a military conquest of the Ukraine. Either she would have to march six hundred miles across Polish territory, to which Poland would naturally object, or if she marched through Czecho-Slovakia would find herself lost in the Carpathian mountains, with no railways or roads, and would still have to violate either Rumanian or Polish territory. The one thing that would save the Soviet, if it is true that it is breaking up, would be an external attack.

The difficulty that Germany and Italy find in dealing with democracies, is that they have no continuity of foreign policy, and therefore States with a stable form of government and a continuity of foreign policy have to be very cautious in their approach to France and Great Britain. France, where the members of the Cabinet are paid their salaries weekly, and Great Britain, where the old policy of continuity of foreign Policy has been abandoned for the pursuit of opposite policies by the Government and the Opposition.

Since the peace pact with Germany was signed, there has been an outburst of attack on Germany, which started **before** the new decrees against the Jews, in the Press, by politicians, and from the pulpit, and Germany is naturally anxiously watching to see whether the next election will return the parties of the Left to power, who would denounce the treaty with Italy, and seek for some pretext to declare war on her.

In every capital in Europe, the triumph of the parties of the Left in this country at the next election, would be taken as the red signal for war.

14

The Hitler Youth Movement

We regret in England, and many Germans with whom I have discussed the matter share the regret, that the German Youth movement so closely following the model of the Boy Scouts, has been made into a separate organization. They told me that more than one imitation of the Boy Scouts movement had been started in Germany and that it was essential at the present stage of the training of the whole country to a new conception of a Nation of people, bound to service and the development of the German national life, to have a separate German organization.

I sympathise with the German point of view and am glad that the friendliest relations have been established and exchange of visiting members arranged, between the two organizations.

The lie has frequently been repeated in this country that the German Youth movement is military in its object and practice. This is an invention of the enemy and is not true.

I owe the following account of the Hitler Youth Movement to Baldur von Schirach.

Nothing is more suited to a friendly exchange of opinion between educationalists of different nations than the matter of youthful upbringing. The more the youth leaders in the various nations of culture succeed in agreeing on certain fundamental points, the more chance there is of our young people growing up in a friendly spirit toward each other instead of antagonistic. In this field of international understanding the aim should not be to effect certain political ideas and maximes but rather the more human aspects, those of mutual respect, comradeship and real sincerity. The more the youth of all nations gets to know each other by means of personal contact the more it will come to respect each other's individualities and to understand existing differences, for each country produces the kind of youth movement expressive of its characteristics and its nature. I am convinced that the Hitler boy, just as the English boy scout and the small fry of the Italian Balila, typifies the essential qualities of his native land.

The National Socialist Youth developed in 1926 out of an enthusiasm felt by a few young Germans for the personality and the ideas of our Führer. The principle laid down in the very beginning - "Youth must be led by youth" - supplies the necessary balance to pure School education by the early shouldering of duties and personal responsibility. The mistakes that may still be found in this system and its possible deficiencies, in my opinion, fade away when faced with the enormous gain resulting from the early development of responsibility and the attendant stimulus to exert all faculties. The key to each situation is efficiency and the efficiency of a young person is no less valuable than that of an older one.

During the development of the Hitler Youth Movement the necessity arose for organized formations. Apart from the fact that the girls were organized from the very beginning in a special body known as the *"B.D.M."* (Association of German Girls), the boys from 10 to 14 grouped under the *"Young Folk"* and from 14 to 18 as the *"Hitler Youth"*, all these were divided up into a special system of units.

The training of leaders for these various units takes place in special training schools which are almost without exception to be found in beautiful surroundings. Here they go in for sport, receive physical training and theoretical instruction in the theory of life with the team spirit pervading everything.

Contrary to many other countries the young people in Germany are not trained in the handling of military effectives. Shooting which is practised to a very small degree only in the training schools for leaders is only with air guns and is a form of sport. Such words as "home", "camp" and "outing" are so much a part of the Hitler boys that I could not fail to touch on them briefly. The homes are as it were clubs providing a place of congregation for the boys and making them independent of cafés and so of alcohol and nicotine. In the "Hour of the Young Nation", broadcast throughout Germany, the uniform spirit is inculcated. By camping is naturally meant tent life which provides an equable balance for the city lads, above all for the industrial workers. The days in camp are spent in play and the evenings round an open space with singing and performances etc. Opportunities are given for swimming and riding. Last year about one million youths slept out in tents and we hope before long that there will be no Hitler boys who have not spent at least three weeks a year out camping. The hiking Hitler youth is afforded cheap night lodgings through a special organization and facilities for sojourn. This is the German Youth Hostel Association. There are some 2,000 hostels scattered throughout the country in castle ruins or old town turrets and the like which are especially maintained for the youthful wanderers [i.e. hikers].

Referring now to the essential political aspect of my organization I should like to point out first and foremost that today as from the beginning the pride of the Hitler Youth is the fact that the young workmen are with us whom we have been struggling to win over for so long. With the advent of the régime the struggle of the National Socialist youth was by no means ended; on the contrary, the hard fight for effecting the claim to totality began and with it the decisive question whether other organizations and units aside from the Hitler Youth should have the right to train the rising generation. National Socialist Germany maintained then as now that outside the schools there should be no educational body in Germany other than the Hitler Youth. This viewpoint was propounded in 1933. At the commencement of 1934 the inclusion of all protestant youth was provisionally completed and outside the Hitler Youth there was only one other youth organization, a catholic one, all other belong to our community, the fellowship of young Germany. Nevertheless, there is a plane on which the confessional organization is essentially justified and recognised by the Hitler Youth. If the former refrains from exerting temporal powers and confines its sphere of influence to matters of the soul I see no reason why there should be no confessional organization of the youth of the country.

And now with reference to something of material importance. Of all the Hitler Youth activities I would like to touch on but one here, namely, the Reich Crafts Competition which the youth of Germany organized in conjunction with the German Labour Front. This is looked upon by the young people as the most idealistic avowal of an entire generation to German Labour. In his *"Wilhelm Meister"* Goethe denoted respect as the keynote to all education. The youth whose leader I have the honour to be is aiming at this ideal in the spirit of the great Master who has named it as the aim of the world youth common to all and uniting all.

When Hitler was reviewing the Hitler youth in Nuremberg the other day he said, giving us a glimpse into the heart and soul of the man, *"How wonderful, how beautiful are the children of Germany".*

15

The Winter Help Organization

Apart from the extreme poverty which seems to haunt our modern civilization especially in large cities, Germany has suffered terribly not only from the war but from the reparation payments; the occupation of the Ruhr which, under the incompetent socialist administration, brought about the flight from the mark ruining thousands of homes; and later on the appalling amount of unemployment.

The National Socialist Party as soon as they came into power decided that the distress, especially in great cities, quite apart from Government relief and work for the unemployed, required the personal touch of a voluntary association and so with characteristic German thoroughness they proceeded to do it. In this as in all other matters where the volunteer worker is wanted, the Nazi organization covering the whole country is of course invaluable.

The aim of the National Socialist Welfare Society is the relief of persons who are physically and mentally sound, but who, in consequence of adverse general conditions, have fallen into a state of distress which threatens the health and development of both themselves and their dependents.

In accordance with this principle of preserving the healthy part of the German Nation, the National Socialist Welfare Society does not help those who are hereditarily diseased or suffering from incurable mental or physical diseases. These persons are cared for by the State.

Any person in Germany may be given relief by the National Socialist Welfare Society, whether he is employed or not. Special attention is paid to persons who are employed but whose wages scarcely suffice to support their large families.

Since the foundation of the Winter Help Scheme, the number of persons assisted has decreased steadily from 16,617,681 in 1933/34 to 13,866,571 in 1934/35 and 12,909,469 in 1935/36 and 10,711,526 in 1936/37, owing to the favourable development of employment and trade in Germany. It is to be noted that these figures include family members.

The National Socialist Welfare Society never distributes money as relief. Relief always takes the form of goods. In this way any possibility of the relief being used for other purposes or unnecessary purchases is avoided. In order to increase the possibility of choice, increasing use has been made of vouchers for food, clothing, electricity, gas and other necessities.

Winter Help Collections

The Winter Help Scheme operates during the six months from October to March which experience has shown to be the most critical period of the year in regard to employment and sustenance. Many seasonal trades have to cease work during a great part of this period owing to inclement weather, and for the unemployed and those in receipt of small pensions the necessity of buying heating materials and winter clothing weighs heavily on a budget already burdened by the normal increase in price of many foodstuffs during winter time.

The Winter Help Organization began in October 1933, with an initial contribution of 15,000,000 marks by the State. It collected not only contributions in kind, but also monetary contributions in many and varied appeals throughout the country, and used the funds collected for large scale buying of the necessities for daily life, thus making the money go considerably further than it would have gone had it been distributed as money.

Apart from the initial gift mentioned, this organization receives no State assistance, and is supported entirely by individual people in Germany, through their contributions and sacrifices. It is a fundamental principle that the contributions must be absolutely voluntary. No one is in the slightest way forced to contribute.

The National Socialist Welfare Society's main sources of income are as follows:

Contributions from individuals. These contributions may be divided into two kinds. First there are those from persons in receipt of wages, who may volunteer a monthly contribution of an amount equal to about 10 per cent of their monthly Wages Tax. This sum is collected by the firm, in so far as the employees have declared their consent. Secondly, those who are not employed, but who have a private income, volunteer contributions in the form of small deductions from their Postal or Bank accounts.

Special advantages are gained through the free transport of coal for the Winter Help given by the German Railways. The transport costs must be paid, but are refunded later.

Contributions by Germans living abroad, which are collected by the Foreign Department of the National Socialist Party.

The proceeds from the "One Pot Meal". On the second Sunday in every month, a simple meal is prepared in all households. The money saved by giving up a more costly meal is forwarded to the Winter Help.

Organization of the Welfare work

1. The National Socialist Welfare Society is organized with the object of helping so far as possible all those in need of relief. This is only possible through a considerable participation of the population in voluntary assistance work.

The "helpers" are thus divided into two classes - those in receipt of salaries or remuneration, and honorary permanent and occasional helpers.

The National Socialist organizations and unions are also called upon to help, as well as other societies dedicated to social work and whose membership is entirely voluntary.

2. The National Socialist Welfare Society is organized in the following unified system:

a) Block Leader. This leader is responsible for social supervision in a block which usually contains three or four tenements. He collects the regular contributions and his most important duty is to ascertain persons in need of assistance and to supervise their relief. This is a difficult and responsible position, as often - especially in the case of the most respectable people - those in distress are reluctant to acknowledge their condition.

All the contributions collected, together with the reports on the position of those in need of relief and further developments are directed to the

b) Cell Leader. This official is in charge of eight to ten blocks, and he gives exact, and where necessary, personal information about the cases reported, to the

c) Local Group. The Local Group also receives all contributions in money and in kind from the cell leader. The Local Group, after consulting the Block and Cell Leaders, decides the relief which must be administered.

d) The District Group, the Regional Group and the Reich administration are competent to administrate the organization of the National Socialist Welfare Society, and to administrate the monetary proceeds.

The District and Regional Groups receive mostly goods presented by business concerns. The District Groups have often stocks of clothing, etc., and the Regional Groups always have supplies. Apart from the smaller relief, such as potatoes, coal and food, given regularly by the Local Group, the Regional Group provides more relief in the form of clothing, shoes, domestic utensils, furniture, and sends people to the country to recover their health. The person in need of relief is provided with the necessities on production of a certificate from his Local Group.

Administration

All the money contributed is administered by the Regional and Reich administration. As mentioned above, no relief is given in the form of money, so these contributions are used to buy large quantities of goods, which makes it possible to obtain considerably lower prices. The difference of these wholesale prices and the retail values of the goods distributed appears as "added value" in the accounts of the Society.

The costs of administration, of wages and compensation for the helpers are extremely small. During the Winter 1936/37 the total costs for salaries, wages, compensation, office work, printing, rent, light, heating etc. came to 1.84 per cent of the total proceeds. The total income for 1936/37 amounted to 387,088,000 marks without the "added value".

This scheme has several good points worthy of our consideration.

In the first place the whole ground of charitable relief is covered by one Society. There is no overlapping.

In the second place the whole of a city is divided into small circles of three or four tenements in charge of the Block Leader, thus enabling the close personal supervision which alleviating real distress requires to prevent fraud.

In the third place the payment is in kind. This does not of course eliminate the sale of food tickets for drink and similar abuses, but it is the best that can be done, and the Block Leader will soon discover such cases of fraud.

The remarkably low administrative expense. The Society has 1,349,008 helpers of whom only 8,652 are paid.

The "One Pot Meal" is an excellent idea and has become universal in Germany. It is a definite reminder of the needs of our poorer brethren and a simple sacrifice in which all participate. It is not only a source or income but has a symbolical meaning and an ethical value.

It is the boast of the Society that in Berlin last Winter not one person was inadequately fed or clothed or without a fire all the winter in one room.

One of the interesting features of National Socialism is that it is developing its own symbolism. The march of the burnished spades, the slowly moving river of the blood red flags in the Stadium in the temple of light, the one pot meal, which will become a social sacrament, are all examples of this symbolism to impress the hearts as well as the minds of the people with a new conception of service one to another.

16

National Socialism and the Protestant Church

A new and living organization is bound to come up against older organizations and some adjustments are necessary. To some extent this has happened between the Protestant sects in Germany and National Socialism. Moreover, Protestantism like Democracy - its political child - is an intensely individualistic religion and consequently it has little sympathy for and understanding of National Socialism.

Because Protestantism is based on the denial of an authority controlling the individual conscience, from the commencement it has divided and sub-divided and tends to resist all attempts at unity of organization. Born and brought up in Scotland, the home of Calvinism, I speak with knowledge.

Recent years have seen a remarkable coming together of the Presbyterian Churches in Scotland, but for years the Church was divided into many sects; divided on points of Church government and minute differences of doctrine, and hell fire was freely sprayed upon the sects which differed on theological matters.

I have never forgotten a sentence from a sermon preached by a Scottish divine, after the two Presbyterian Churches, the Free Church and the United Presbyterian Church had agreed to combine. A minority of

THE CASE FOR GERMANY.

the Free Church ministers objected and formed a Church of their own, and one of them preaching about the men who had been his fellow ministers and friends a few weeks before spoke as follows:

> "Below the Heathen and below the Roman Catholics on the very floor of hell which is watered by the tears of those of moderate opinions, will be found the ministers of the United Free Church."

With these experiences behind me I confess I listen with some scepticism to the attacks made on the National Socialist Government, which has undoubtedly burnt its fingers in trying to produce unity among sects whose very life lies in disunion.

The troubles in the Protestant Church in Germany, as the following brief historical resumé will show, began before the advent of National Socialism and the new Government had to face difficulties already existing.

Hitler feels that Protestantism, which originated in Germany, is especially and peculiarly the type of Christianity which has become the national faith of the German people, and is most desirous to see it working in harmony with the National Socialist State. To-day some 80 per cent of the Churches are working in harmony with the Government. A section refuse to administer the simple regulations of the Government and attack it violently from the pulpit, and obtain much satisfaction from a quite unnecessary martyrdom when fined or sent to a concentration camp. **The Government have not the remotest desire or intention to interfere with the religious teaching and faith of the Church.** The Protestant Churches have always been part of the State and some external organization and financial arrangements are necessary for efficient administration.

To take a simple instance. Every German on registration has to declare his confession or to prove he never belonged to one or has resigned from membership. He has then to subscribe a fixed amount every year, which is collected by the State and redistributed to the Churches along with State grants.

The National Socialist State since January 30, 1933, has through its state organs, placed the following sums accruing from public taxes, at the disposal of both Churches:

Financial year 1933 .... RM. 130 million
financial year 1934 .... RM. 170 million
financial year 1935 .... RM. 250 million
financial year 1936 .... RM. 320 million
financial year 1937 .... RM. 400 million
financial year 1938 .... RM. 500 million.

To the above sums must be added approximately RM. 85 million per annum of additional payments made by the various German states, and a further RM. 7 million per annum from the parishes and parish unions, as well as 300 million marks which the churches obtain as annual rent from their landed property.

If a member wishes to leave a congregation he pays two years' subscription on retiring from membership. It has been the custom to read out the names of these backsliders from the pulpit. The Government has forbidden this in the name of freedom of conscience. Niemöller and his followers refuse to obey this reasonable regulation. At the time when the Berlin correspondent was filling columns in *The Times* about this gentleman his followers had dwindled to about a thousand persons.

Under "Protestantism", in the wider meaning of the word, is understood not only the Churches and Confessions of Faith founded on the Lutheran Reformation, but also those founded by the Swiss reformers Calvin and Zwingli. Both together include about sixty-five per cent of those who adhere to the Christian faith in Germany.

The result of the various reformations in so far as the attitude of the Church towards the State was concerned, was the Peace of Augsburg of

1555, which stipulated that the subjects of each State had to accept the creed of their sovereign ("CUIUS REGIO EIUS RELIGIO").

This decision not only widened the gulf between the Roman Catholic and Protestant religions, but also split the Protestant Church into various Lutheran and Calvinist sections, through the system called "Sovereign Determination of the Church" *("Landesherrliches Kirchenregiment")*. This expression really meant that the boundaries of the various Protestant Churches corresponded with those of the German States (Federal States, Principalities), and that the rulers of these States were also the highest authorities in their respective Churches ("PRINCEPS SUMMUS EPISCOPUS").

After the abdication of these rulers, in consequence of the revolution of 1918, the Regional Churches, which numbered in all twenty-eight, were faced with the necessity of creating a new organization. In view of the disappearance of the former local rulers and highest Church authorities, the Regional Churches adopted a kind of democratic constitution, similar to the democratic constitution of Weimar, but perhaps also influenced by early Christian ideas. The administration was divided into three bodies:

1. The Church Assembly, composed of Church Members.
2. The Church Delegates.
3. The Church Government.

The actual nomenclature varied in the different States.

No further separation of the Church from the State was carried through, least of all on the financial side. Stress was however laid on the principle that the Church boundaries need not necessarily coincide with the frontiers of the State. For example, the Evangelical Churches of Danzig and of Posen (now Poznan in the Republic of Poland) belong at present to the Evangelical Church of the Old Prussian Union, the former State Church of Prussia.

As far as internal organization is concerned, numerous efforts had already been made in the nineteenth century to unite German Protestantism, which had been split up into twenty-eight Regional Churches. These efforts were revived after 1918, and 1921 led to the foundation of the "German Evangelical Church Federation" which was to represent the interests of all Protestants in Germany. The Church Federation was a union of the twenty-eight Regional Churches, which were otherwise entirely independent in doctrine, constitution and administration.

The experience of the Great War produced a development generally known as the "Lutheran Renaissance" in the religious realm of German Protestantism. This was chiefly concerned with a new interpretation of Luther's doctrine and personality, a movement which had already originated with the gradual publication of the new edition of Luther's works since 1883.

For years a number of young Church leaders have been trying, in despair of the weak democratic state of the postwar years, to secure a powerful position for the Protestant Church in public life, with the slogan "More Public Influence for the Church" *("Öffentlichkeitswille der Kirche")*.

Until 1933, the usual three groups "left, centre and right" existed within the various "Parliaments" of the Regional Protestant Churches. There were sub-divisions in each of these groups so that the various Church "Parliaments" were divided into about ten different groups.

But a large number of Church members remained completely indifferent to these party fights, and did not feel they were at all represented by any of the groups mentioned. Furthermore, the German worker had become more and more estranged from Christianity since the end of the nineteenth century, and this was mostly caused by Marxist propaganda.

During the National Socialist revolution, the former political parties of the Weimar republic became superfluous and either dissolved of their own accord or were dissolved by the National Socialist leadership. These events were bound to affect Protestant Church members. There was no outside influence exerted on them, but as the same people are members of the State and of the Church, political developments could not fail to influence the Church situation. This resulted in a new "alignment" of Church "Party" groups.

All the former Church Parties were amalgamated in the course of the year 1933, and united in a group which was first known as "Gospel and Church" *(Evangelium und Kirche)*, but is now represented by the so-called "Confessional Front" *(Bekenntnisfront)*.

In opposition to this union of former Church Parties arose the former neutral section of Church members. They felt that a time had come, when all current Church questions could be settled on the same way as the political problems. A large group of Protestants with a positive attitude towards National Socialism formed a Church Party based on this conviction, called **"German Christians"** *(Deutsche Christen)*. This Party was actually founded in 1932. During the course of further developments in 1933, the "German Christians" split up in two main sub-divisions which may be characterised as follows:

a) The Old Movement, led by Joachim Hossenfelder. This movement feels responsible for the reorganization of the life of the nation according to National Socialist principles, and regards the Church as a special organization within the framework of the State. The theology of this movement may be described as essentially liberal.

b) The New Movement, based on the teachings of Emanuel Hirsch of Göttingen and Karl Fezer of Tübingen. They are not striving to adopt the organization of the Church to the exact political forms of National Socialism, but they seek an independent revival of Protestantism through the actual teaching of Luther. They are thus closely connected with the Luther Renaissance Movement described above.

These three movements, the size of which is difficult to estimate, resulted in the following developments.

After great difficulties, the Church succeeded in arranging elections and a National Synod was formed in September 1933. This Synod accepted a unified Reich Church Constitution and elected a Reich Bishop, Ludwig Müller. This Reich Church Constitution is a framework for a Federal Organization and not very different from that of the former German Evangelical Church Federation. It is still recognized by all groups.

Towards the end of 1933, the differences between the two main Protestant groups grew more acute. The "New Movement" of the German Christians tried to bring the situation under Church control by nominating Professor Beyer of Greifswald as Minister for Church Affairs. This attempt proved however unsuccessful.

The Prussian Ministerial Secretary Jäger, a member of the Civil Service, was now appointed to the Church Government by the Reich Bishop Müller. Jäger was thus not appointed by the State, but by the Church Government.

As Legal Administrator of the Reich Church, he tried, through revolutionary methods, to bring the independent Regional Churches under the centralized control of the Reich Church. This meant depriving the Regional Churches concerned of their independence.

In face of these attempts, the Confessional Front aligned itself with the Regional Churches against centralized control, and organized itself more firmly in the so-called "Opposition Movement". This movement included the Regional Churches, of Bavaria (Bishop Meiser), Württemberg (Bishop Wurm), and Hanover (Bishop Mahrahrens) and also received growing support from other Regional Churches.

The Opposition Movement claimed further to be the only true Protestant Church, and demanded the sole leadership of German Protestantism on the ground that the Church was in a state of emergency. The German Christians opposed this claim to exclusive power.

After the resignation of Jäger, the State intervened on account of the State of emergency in the Church, as the internal peace of the Nation was threatened, and a re-establishment of the financial and legal conditions in the Church did not seem possible without the help of the State. In 1935, Hitler proclaimed a "Law to secure the Existence of the German Evangelical Church." Through this Law a special Ministry for Church Affairs was created and the newly appointed Hanns Kerrl was included in the Cabinet as Church Minister. He was empowered to issue decrees "to create a state of order which would make it possible for the Church to govern itself in all freedom and peace, in questions regarding faith and doctrine."

Kerrl formed a Reich Church Committee from men in the Church, which should govern the Evangelical Church during a two-years' transition period. At the moment this Reich Church Committee, with its various sub-committees, is the only institution in the administration of the Church which is recognized by the State. The State has not given exclusive recognition to either the German Christians or to the Confessional Front, but only to the union of both in the Church Committees.

The introduction of a Ministry for Church Affairs, under Herr Kerrl, and its activities up till now, show that the State does not intend to influence in one way or another the religious problem and the Church struggle within the Evangelical Church. The aim of the State is to reach a solution of the current questions through Protestantism itself.

These principles of the State's policy are very much to be welcomed from the Protestant point of view. Protestantism has indeed every interest in solving its problem of its own accord, and through its own spiritual development, instead of having this solution decided, perhaps through force, by an authority with no deep feelings in this particular matter.

All Protestant groups who have a real will to constructive co-operation and who are at all interested in a natural solution of the Church situation, are therefore working actively in the Church Committee.

A great part of the German Christians has already consented to co-operate in the Church Committee. The main body is now divided into two rather different groups.

The greater part of the so-called Confessional Front, under the leadership of the Regional Bishop of Hanover, Dr. Mahrahrens, has also agreed to co-operate in the Church Committee.

The radical section of the Confessional Front, led by Pastor Niemöller, will have nothing to do with the Church Committee on principle, and refuses to co-operate in it. These radical Confessionalists have hitherto been unable to find a way of approach to Nationalist Socialist principles and are therefore incapable of understanding the national revival in Germany.

This negative attitude can become dangerous. **When religious reasons are used as a pretext for a struggle against the State itself, the State has the duty to take the necessary measures to secure internal peace within the nation.**

Unfortunately, these events have been represented abroad in a way which greatly exaggerates their actual importance. They do not result, as has been assumed, from a spiritual struggle between Protestantism and the State, but are only individual conflicts, on the detail of Church Government, between certain parsons and the State, with which the great majority of Church members and the Church itself have nothing to do.

From the German Christians the different groups of the "German Faith movement" *(Deutsche Glaubensbewegung)* must be clearly distinguished. They are much discussed abroad under the name "New Heathens".

This movement has nothing to do with the Christian Churches or with Christianity in general, and wishes to found a belief in God on the traditions of the German race and history. These people cannot be described simply as atheists.

The German Faith Movement had at first a great success. Today it is already declining rapidly.

It is also clear that problems arise for the existing Confessions, not on account of pure dogmatism, whether Christian or not, but on account of the actual experience of the present day political life of the German Nation.

A solution of these problems will have to be attempted between the various Protestant groups and will perhaps determine their future attitude towards each other.

This fruitful struggle of ideas and their protagonists may go on for decades. Its ultimate results cannot be foreseen in detail. But its effect will almost certainly be a deep-rooted religious revival of the German Nation.

17

Economics

"Why kill Germans when we can starve them."
Senator Pittman.

The post war period is one in which economics have gone mad and the most extraordinary things are done by Governments. In Brazil the Government throws thousands of tons of coffee beans into the sea while the consumer in this country is paying 2/6 to 3/- a lb. for beans which merely require to be brought to his door; and the Government of the USA. has paid farmers large subsidies not to grow food and let the land go derelict, while millions of unemployed are starving. In this country while it is admitted that one third of the population is underfed, the farmer is ploughing his potatoes into the land, and millions of fish are being thrown into the sea to keep up prices in the Billingsgate market. Last summer in the south of England the magnificent plum crop was left to rot on the trees, and in Cambridgeshire where the smallholder was getting ½ for 12 lbs. of carefully picked and packed Victoria plums, the retail shopkeeper in London 40 miles away was getting 8d. a lb.

We are told in the papers that the chicken farmer is being ruined, yet a chicken costs 1/- to ½ per lb. in London with all the offal weighed in and charged for at the same rate.

Not only does Nature give us of her abundance as never before in the history of mankind owing to improvements in agriculture, but the engineer has invented marvellous means of transport - and yet the people are not fed.

Just as it is abhorrent to the German Government and the German people to see an idle man on the dole, so the modern economics which destroys food to keep up prices and fines heavily the man who grows more than his quota, is contrary to their economic principle. Hitler has said, "I am no student of modern economics, and I must believe that the German who by his labour produces an article of use, such as food, has enriched and not impoverished the Reich". The implication is that what is needed to secure the food supply of a Nation is direction not destruction, and the first essential is to use the middle man for his proper function for which his experience fits him, - the distribution of food at a modest percentage to pay for his services. He can no longer rig the market in Germany, and force down prices for the farmer and force up prices for the consumer.

It is said, I know not with what truth, that a cabbage passes through the hands of twelve merchants between the farmer and the consumer in this country.

The problem of the proper distribution of food is no easy one and I discussed it with Germans over there, but they are satisfied that while adjustments may be necessary they are working on the right lines. The peasant farmer is as satisfied as any farmer would ever be, and the men, women and children in every quarter of Nuremberg, which is a small German Birmingham, look far better fed than in this country.

To give the farmer a sufficient living and feed the people is the first duty of the modern State.

There is another modern economic delusion which is not accepted in Germany, that work, especially manual work, is a curse, and that modern inventions should enable men to idle for 20 hours out of 24. Germany has not found it so. It is by hard work that she has been lifted out of the economic pit. Ask the boys in the Labour Camps if they would change the struggle with Nature, the use of pick and shovel, for sitting in a cinema watching a film, or packed in a crowd watching paid athletes play football, and they will laugh at you. Compare him, hardy and brown with the sun, marching singing through the streets, with our anaemic physically undeveloped city youth loafing with a fag in his mouth.

In dealing with the problem of the staple articles of food the German Government has fixed a price for the farmer, and a price for the consumer, and while the middle man distributes, the State supervises and arranges to deal with the distribution when there is a shortage in one part of the country and an excess in another. The importation of food is regulated according to demand, and the duty paid equalizes the price with the internal price. Owing to the fact that so large a proportion of the land is in the hands of the peasant proprietor, they are not faced with our problem that any increase of profit to the farmer soon leaves his pocket in the form of rent or excessive interest to the Bank. The assistance of extra labour for seasons when labour is short on the land is arranged, and many of the temporary assistants become permanent land workers. When land has been reclaimed or formerly unfarmed land is being broken up for cultivation the State provides the new settler with capital.

They have found it impossible to fix prices for perishable foodstuffs, and have divided Germany into districts, the perishable foodstuffs being collected at a centre and redistributed from there.

They claim that this has proved a success, securing the consumer from excessive prices and protecting the producer from a loss. The handling of perishable foodstuffs is one of our most serious economic problems, the grower frequently selling at a loss, while the price of perishable foodstuffs in our cities is much too high for the poor man's family to eat the quota of vegetables and fruit which is necessary for health. As I have said elsewhere, in devising the four years' plan the Government is not satisfied even with this organization, putting the wastage of food at 1500 million marks a year, one half of which takes place during distribution.

With our haphazard method of collecting and distributing and utterly inadequate markets and myriads of small greengrocers, with no proper methods of storage anywhere, the wastage must be enormous, and largely accounts for the excessive price to the consumer.

In Germany every encouragement is given to the allotment holder, with a view to the people in towns growing their own supplies. I have mentioned elsewhere the cheapness and excellence of the food in German restaurants.

The system of magnificent motor roads, the construction of which is being vigorously pushed on, will help the matter of perishable food distribution still further. One of the absurd falsehoods which is repeated at intervals is that these roads are being built solely for military purposes. They are being built for sound economic reasons, but would doubtless prove very useful in a defensive war enabling troops to be quickly concentrated on any frontier. It is unnecessary to enlarge on the economic problem raised by fixed prices which is a complete departure from the economic principle of supply and demand and an open market, but they claim in Germany that they have found - as we have found - that the open market fails as a method of food distribution, and they seem to have been much more successful than our Milk, Potato and Bacon Boards. The probable reason is that owing to our love of compromise, we have combined the evils of a competitive system with the evils of a socialistic experiment, without getting the benefits of either. Either have a free market, or fix prices right through from producer to consumer.

It must be remembered that Germany has the advantage of having educated the people to a new ideal of service upon which they can call, which makes all the difference between failure and success. The desire is to assist these experiments and not try and find how to use them for private aggrandizement. To say that all the German people have grasped the idea of social service would be absurd, but their education in a new conception of social order is being vigorously carried on, and behind all is the stern necessity of making both ends meet for the whole Nation.

We are so overflowing with the wealth of the world, though we share it round so unequally, that we think we can afford to be extravagant.

Their method of organizing the distribution of perishable food is well worth the study of the Ministry of Agriculture as it is one of our most serious economic problems to-day.

Finance

A series of articles attacking different aspects of National Socialism were published in *The Banker* two years ago. One is on the finance of the National Socialist Government, based on certain official figures. These articles are the only detailed examination of German finance by an expert, and therefore is made the basis of this chapter.

This article reveals a strong bias against Germany, a bias which is still more reflected in the introduction to the series of hostile articles in *The Banker*, an introduction which consists of a most ignorant and violent attack on the National Socialist Government.

In spite of the bias the actual figures given in the article prove an excellent defence of National Socialist Finance, and I propose to discuss them in this chapter.

The Two Problems

When the National Socialist Government came into power they were faced with two problems, which required for their solution a large capital expenditure - namely, the necessity for reducing to reasonable figures the huge number of unemployed, amounting to 6,000,000, and the pressing necessity of arming the German people for defence, surrounded as they are by nations spending larger and larger sums on armaments and increasing the number of soldiers on a peace footing.

THE CASE FOR GERMANY.

A government has two sources of money: increased taxation and borrowing. In this country the Government adopts two methods of borrowing, Treasury Bills and loans over long periods. From time to time a portion of the indebtedness under Treasury Bills is converted into a permanent loan.

We have found it necessary in order to bring our armaments up to the standard set in France and Russia to face an expenditure of £1,500,000,000. France claims to-day to have the most powerful and best equipped army in Europe, the Soviet have 2,000,000 men on a peace footing and 6,000 bombing planes, and Germany by tremendous efforts can claim to have an army to-day sufficient for defence, which is all that she aims at having.

When we find it necessary to expend £1,500 millions merely to bring our existing armaments up to the modern level, it is evident that, beginning from nothing, Germany had a tremendous task.

The most urgent problem before the German Government was the unemployed, and before plunging into armament expenditure she tried to persuade France to accept a reduced number of men on a peace footing. Her proposals to do this were rejected.

There are two ways of dealing with the unemployed problem. One, the easier, is to pay them out of taxation a dole sufficient to keep them alive.

This has been our method since the War and has cost us hundreds of millions with nothing to show for it.

We have occasionally undertaken public works in a sporadic and inefficient manner, resulting in wastage of public money with nothing to show for it commensurate with the expenditure. The other method is to carry out public works which will increase the capital wealth of the nation on a well-thought-out plan.

There is a great deal of capital expenditure which can be undertaken only by the State, as it would yield a doubtful profit to private enterprise and would require a vast capital. It is impossible to assess exactly the increase in wealth due to such expenditure.

Roads

It has from earliest times been the task of the State to make and maintain roads and to carry out vast schemes of land drainage, irrigation and land reclamation.

From the first clearances made by primitive man in the primeval forest, land reclamation has never paid on a strict accountant basis, but it has paid the people a thousandfold through the centuries.

One man in this country, Mr. Lloyd George, has advocated for years expenditure on public works. He pointed out among other things the necessity of up-to-date arterial roads, and the danger of the long neglect of land drainage in this country.

The recent disastrous floods in the Fens involving an expenditure of many millions if the Fen country is to be saved, is due to this neglect, and we are just beginning to deal with the question of arterial roads.

Sweden's Example

The little country of Sweden adopted the plan of public works and is to-day the most prosperous country in Europe.

The German Government decided on a bold policy of public works. They are constructing throughout Germany magnificent arterial roads for motor traffic; they have reclaimed vast areas of land; they have undertaken great schemes of building and reconstruction; and have spent money in various other ways of permanent benefit to the German people.

In five years they have reduced unemployment from 6,000,000 to nothing and have set up and equipped an army on a peace footing of 500,000 men. They are now proceeding to develop still further the

THE CASE FOR GERMANY.

internal resources of Germany under the four years' plan, and to-day they are hiring labour from Italy and Holland.

Let me now return, from this long digression, to the financial problem.

In Great Britain, owing to the vast reserves of capital a Government can always float a permanent loan.

Germany, bled white by reparations and the vast confiscations after the War by the victorious allies, and heavily indebted by outside borrowing at exorbitant rates of interest, could not do that, although her internal war debt had been wiped out under the Socialist regime by a vast depreciation of currency.

The bold device adopted by the German Government was for the State to finance this large expenditure trusting to the economic recovery of Germany to take over this expenditure. This device has been fully justified by results, the expenditure being gradually converted into short term loans, corresponding to our Treasury Bills, followed by long term loans. The plan adopted is regarded as somewhat unorthodox by the writer of the article in *The Banker*, but he admits that owing to the control exercised over the banking system and finance in Germany it has been possible to do this without the consequences that usually follow such a policy - a rise in prices, and that the talk of approaching bankruptcy is absurd.

Taking as a reference figure the Budget of the year 1932, the expenditure was 6,700 million marks, the figures for

1933-4 are 9,700 million marks
1934-5 are 12,200 million marks
1935-6 are 16,700 million marks
1936-7 are 18,800 million marks,

showing a net increase of 31,100 million marks for these four years or £ 2,500 millions.

Steady Rise

The yield of taxation during the period has been 9,800 million marks above that of 1932, rising steadily and progressively from year to year, and owing to other sources of income less than half this amount had to be raised by loans, a total indebtedness which is not large for a country of the population of Germany, and may be compared with our figure of over £8,000 million sterling.

In order to make as impressive a figure as possible, the writer of the article in *The Banker* charges the whole of the sum of 31,000 million marks to the armaments account alone, and draws an entirely fictitious budget for 1936-7.

He ignores the large expenditure on public works which comes out of this total, the fact that the Government has not only met the interest on external debt but paid off one-third of the external debt and the increase of annual expenditure required for the civil service, the maintenance of the army on a peace footing and the extension of the social services.

The National Socialist Government has resisted the easy way out of their economic and exchange difficulties by borrowing abroad after the manner of other European countries. France has just borrowed £50 millions from us and proposes to borrow more.

This policy of self-sufficiency, or, as our Press call it, "economic isolation", is, perhaps, a reason of the unpopularity of Germany in the City, the world's biggest moneylender, an unpopularity which is reflected in our Press and in *The Banker*.

When our Government announced an expenditure of £1,500 millions to bring our armaments up to the level of other European countries, the public were astounded at the enormous cost of the equipment of a modern army and navy.

In the light of these figures the total expenditure by the German Government under all heads of £2,500 millions is not excessive even though the whole had been devoted to rebuilding a navy and equipping an army of 500,000 men up to the standard of the armies of France and Russia.

As an actual fact, 15,000 million marks have been spent on other purposes than on armaments.

The total amount borrowed is not excessive and the success of the capital expenditure is proved by the growing internal prosperity of Germany and the elimination of unemployment.

In fact the figures confirm the conclusion come to by other observers, that Germany has been satisfied to create and equip an army sufficient for defence, and has no projects of foreign conquest.

Since this date Germany has been compelled most unwillingly to fresh expenditure on armaments owing to the vast sums being spent by Great Britain and France as it is impossible to trust the foreign policies of Democracies. Daladier has just been saved by 9 votes and if at the next election here the Labour Party came in they would probably take the first opportunity to force war on Germany.

The difficult position in which Germany is placed by the heavy reparations she had to pay, forcing her to borrow money outside at high rates of interest, has never been properly appreciated in this country. When she had been bled to the last sixpence, and her economic ruin completed by the occupation of the Ruhr, she was left with a heavy external debt which had to be repaid some time and on which the interest was due. In spite of her economic distress she has never adopted the facile expedient of repudiating her debt, and has paid off one third of the capital sum. We cancelled a thousand millions of the debt France owed to us, and also cancelled large sums due from Italy and Belgium, and we still owe four hundred millions to the United States and are neither repaying the capital nor paying the interest. The Soviet not only repudiated the debt of the former government, but confiscated wholesale the property of companies in Russia financed by foreign capital. It has been usual for countries after a revolution to repudiate the debts of the former government, and the Nazi government might well have followed this practice; on the contrary they assumed the whole burden, have done their best to pay the interest due, and have also taken over the Austrian debt on a reduction of interest of their own debt being agreed to. Other countries besides those mentioned have failed to meet either capital or interest since the war, and Germany is one of the very few countries who faced financial ruin as a result of the war and who are honestly meeting their obligations to the best of their ability.

They have also not adopted the device of depreciating their currency which has been done by so many other countries, having restored the gold mark after the disastrous financial crash.

Having to meet their foreign commitments, and having been deprived of their last ounce of gold by their foreign creditors, they have to control very strictly exports and imports and to prevent any capital leaving Germany. They have also been compelled by their financial position to enter bargains with foreign countries by which they exchange goods directly for goods, and in order to make the plan workable the bargain has to be made to cover several years. This has been described by Mr. Hudson in the House of Commons as an unfair method of trading and he has advised an economic war against Germany to compel them to abandon this method of trading which is forced upon them by their creditors in the city of London and in New York. Dr. Schacht has himself told us that he considers this method of trading "horrible", and said that if Germany could come to some arrangement with her creditors she would adopt unrestricted trading like other countries. It is surely obvious that a buyer and seller have a right to make any bargain they choose, and that no method of trading can be described as unfair. Mr. Hudson was also mistaken in saying that the German government was subsidising the sale of their goods abroad and was by her policy lowering the standard of living in Germany, the attempt to calculate the values of this exchange of goods for goods by converting into sterling being quite misleading.

Germany has not only had a political revolution but has carried out an economic revolution in her method of calculating wealth. All other countries still adopt gold as their standard but Germany, deprived of gold, is calculating wealth in terms of labour production, a new method which is worthy of the study of economists.

When the Nazi party came into power they adopted the very bold policy of putting everyone to work by means of government credits. The result of this policy has been very remarkable. The government money being used to promote vast schemes of road building and land reclamation, the demand of these men for food and other products stimulated other industries and the national income increased so rapidly, that it has been possible to convert this government credit into loans based upon savings, and today far from having any unemployed, Germany has had to import labour, while by every figure by which the prosperity of a country can be tested the national wealth is steadily rising.

When they first proposed to provide work by means of government credit, they were told by the economists that this would result in an immediate rise of prices, but owing to the control of prices exercised by the government no such rise in prices has taken place. At every stage in these bold and new economic experiments the economists have prophesied disaster, and have been proved to be wrong. Dr. Schacht has told us that this economic policy would have been quite impossible unless the German people had first been converted to the Nazi doctrine, and were therefore willing to help the government by loyally carrying out their wishes, instead of making private profit out of the difficulties of the government.

Moreover, while other nations are spending more and more on armaments, Germany is directing her efforts to increasing the productivity of her soil, and the development of new and valuable products which the genius of her chemists is extracting synthetically from her two raw materials - coal and wood.

We find therefore that, after the author of the article in *The Banker* has written his worst against the German government, he has made out an excellent case for her financial policy and dispelled the wild rumours of an excessive expenditure on armaments.

The most recent figures for Germany reveal an increasing prosperity and increasing revenue from taxation. Borrowing by the Government is strictly limited by the amount required to pay interest out of taxation.

The Monopoly of Raw Materials

The graph on the opposite page makes it possible to see at a glance the monopoly of raw materials which is held by the British and French and Dutch Empires, the U.S.A. and the U.S.S.R.

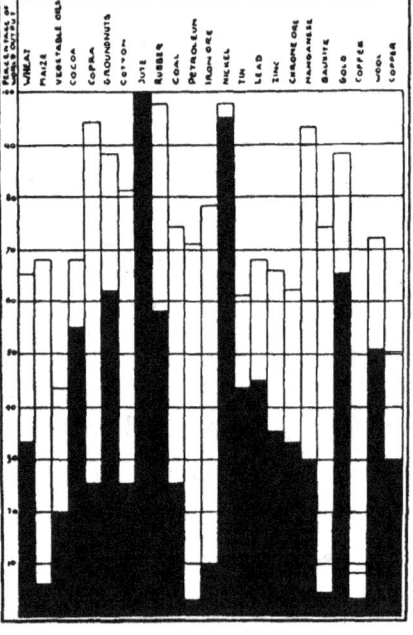

Striking as this diagram is, it does not tell the whole story, because countries outside these are largely financed by British and American capital.

The Argentine, for instance, is at present largely in the hands of British and U.S.A. capitalists.

Other nations wishing to buy raw materials are therefore faced by several difficulties.

In the first place they find a barrier of hostile tariffs against the sale of the goods with which they wish to buy raw materials.

In the second place they find preferential agreements like the Ottawa Agreement.

In the third place they find combines to limit supplies.

The columns give the percentages of the world's raw materials produced by the British, French and Dutch Empires, the U.S.S.R. and the U.S.A. The black portions represent the percentages produced in the British Empire.

These combines are of two kinds. There are government combines, like the tin combine arranged by our government with the governments of the tin producing countries.

THE CASE FOR GERMANY.

And there are commercial combines, like that of the copper producers, for the limitation of output.

The world's oil supplies are in the hands of some three or four big companies which arrange together the price of petrol and of other oils they produce.

We own practically the whole of the world's output of nickel, which is worked by one financial organization with British and American capital.

We, Russia and the U.S.A. possess practically the whole of the world's production of gold.

It may be argued that, for example with tin, the German buyer and the British buyer both have to pay a monopoly price. But, as the British seller lives across the street, what we lose on the swings we make on the roundabouts. We are transferring money from one pocket to another.

Nations like Germany are not in that position.

The conference on raw materials is a meeting of monopolists to discuss their monopoly and is of as much practical value as the disarmament conferences.

The question of raw materials is an international question, in that there are monopolies held by some nations to the impoverishment of other nations.

Monopolies within a nation can be dealt with by the people of that nation, but world-wide monopolies in which groups of nations are plundering other nations is a policy of modern world-wide finance for which no solution has been suggested, or rather the obvious solution will be passed unanimously as a pious opinion but will have no possible practical result, the nations owning the monopolies having not only enormous capital reserves, but overwhelming military forces.

The main business of politicians is to create false issues to deceive the people and President Roosevelt did so the other day when referring to the China-Japanese war, when he proclaimed that the World issue is between Peace loving Democracies and aggressive nations who are in favour of war.

The main issue in the World to-day is the old primitive issue - the need for food.

The World monopoly of raw materials, controlled principally by the British Empire and international financial interests, which are held principally in Great Britain and the U.S.A., is creating a serious economic problem in many nations of which three are most prominent to-day - Japan, Germany and Italy - but France and Russia naturally stand in with us. I have already mentioned the attempt of Italy to find an open door by the conquest of Abyssinia forced upon her by England and France.

Japan is fighting in China to obtain extended markets for her manufactures.

The problem is, as I have said, the primitive one of food, and Japan, Germany and Italy are the three nations of the first rank who form the triple spearhead for a world demand for free trade in raw materials.

For the possessing nations to meet and reprove Japan is pure hypocrisy. The Abyssinian war was forced on Italy, and the Chinese war forced on Japan by the Empires and by international financial control of necessary supplies, and unless a World war is to come, their reasonable demands will have to be met.

The monetary system existing in the world before the war was simple. All money was based on gold and paper or token coinage in every country in the world except China, was interchangeable for a certain weight of gold, and the amount of paper notes issued had a certain fixed ratio to gold reserve.

The reasons for selecting gold are the durability of the metal, the large gold reserve - the accumulation of centuries - and the scarcity of the metal as an ore and cost of extracting, the result being that the output each year did not increase by a large amount the quantity of gold in use. The Mint bought all the gold offered them and converted it into gold coins which were freely used.

It had been possible to handle the increasing trade of the world partly by the printing of paper money, and partly by the increasing use of promises to pay, or cheques.

During the war the whole system was abandoned, and the war financed by the creation of credit and the printing of paper notes as required. Since the war the coinage of gold has never been resumed, and there is no necessary connection between gold reserves and the number of notes issued, we having just abandoned the last residue of such a control. Vast quantities of gold are being accumulated by the U.S.A., France and Great Britain, gold is being mined in larger quantities than ever before and the price of gold measured in sterling is always rising.

In the case of the paper franc and the paper dollar, they have a fixed value in terms of gold but they cannot be exchanged for gold at the national bank. There is no fixed ratio in terms of gold for the pound sterling. The French Government has had repeatedly to alter the ratio between the paper franc and gold, depreciating their currency more and more.

Gold reserves have some value to a country as the gold can be sold in small quantities at the current price to another country to settle debts, and is still used in that way; but obviously if a large quantity of the gold reserves were thrown on the market gold would drop rapidly in price and the "gold is wealth" delusion would vanish never to return; consequently Great Britain, France, and the U.S.A. cannot part with their vast stores of gold which has merely a fictitious value which is not realisable. In case of war involving the three democracies, if they tried to utilise the gold it would lose its value.

To return to paper money, if we imagine an entirely self-contained country with no external trade the amount of paper money in circulation is a matter of indifference as far as prices are concerned, as earnings would have to be at once adjusted to change of prices. It would also obviously be necessary to adjust interest and rent. If before inflation one pound bought twenty loaves of bread and after inflation one pound bought only ten loaves of bread, wages, salaries, interest and rent would have to be adjusted accordingly.

As far as it is possible to discover any intelligible policy on the part of our Government the aim has been, since we abandoned our attempt to return to gold, to keep the cost of living fairly level. The abandonment of gold and the drop of the pound from twenty to fourteen shillings measured against gold produced no change in our economic life.

The problems arise when the self-contained country begins to trade with other countries. Trade consists of the exchange of goods for goods and their price in terms of a fixed standard roughly approximates to the cost of production in each country, and if there is a common measure of money such as existed before the war, the process of barter settles the amount of an article to be exchanged for so much gold, but since the war as the value of money in terms of gold fluctuates in different countries, the exchange of goods is no longer a simple matter. If for instance owing to printing paper money it now takes two pounds instead of one pound to buy twenty loaves, while in the other country it takes twenty francs which were equivalent to one pound before the inflation, the franc is now worth two shillings instead of one shilling in the new currency.

As the money of each country is only legal tender in that country, trade involves two transactions - the exchange of goods and the purchase of the money in the one country with the money in the other country to settle the account, and the relative value of money in the two countries is constantly fluctuating.

In order to obtain some approach to stability in prices, France, Great Britain and the U.S.A. have entered into an arrangement to try and keep the value ratios of the pound sterling, franc and dollar approximately the same, and the British Government has put aside £ 500 millions which is used to buy and sell gold, pounds sterling, and the money of other countries in an attempt to keep the ratios fairly stable. Their transactions are secret and of course might end in disaster if a big world slump took place or war broke out.

THE CASE FOR GERMANY.

It is not too much to say that those responsible for finance in the various countries in the world have no longer any clear understanding of what they are doing in a mass of complicated transactions in values which are purely fictitious. To take an example, the Bank of England buying gold at the current price, entered it in the books at the old value of the sovereign. The Bank has now decided to write up the value of the gold they hold to the market price, and seem to think that by a book entry they have raised the wealth stored in the Bank by some hundreds of millions.

Another big war would bring the whole fictitious system crashing down.

The result of these fictitious systems of currency and the piling up of tariffs, quotas and restrictions on trade, has been a series of financial crises in France, the two million unemployed in this country, the eleven million unemployed in the U.S.A., and distress in more distant parts of the world like Burma where the peasants are starving.

Each economist has a new theory of money more elaborate than the last which all his fellow economists attack.

Germany, when the Nazi party came into power, was in the position of having been stripped of all outside investments, of all gold, and in addition being heavily in debt to the financiers in outside countries for money borrowed to pay reparations.

The new Government would have been quite justified in doing what other revolutionaries had done and repudiated the external debt, and it might have been better for Germany and the outside world if she had done so. Other war debts have been repudiated right and left. France has never attempted to pay what she was owing after we had let her off a thousand millions, and we are not even paying the interest on our debt to America. Germany alone had been an honest debtor and is paying for it.

With no gold, no foreign exchange, six million unemployed and starving farmers she determined to go back to the fundamental principles of economics which have been lost sight of by the financiers of other countries. One thing she was determined on. Not to go into the world financial market and borrow money ever again.

This is the real quarrel that we and the U.S.A., the two big moneylenders, have with her. If she came to the "city" to borrow £100 millions all the attacks in the Press, the denunciations on platforms, the utilization of the fugitive Jew as a political stunt would stop. The City pulls the strings and the Press obey.

The fundamental principles are that wealth is the product of labour applied to raw materials to make articles of utility. Labour may be employed to make goods for immediate consumption, or to increase capital values by carrying out work which will enable more articles of utility to be produced at a lower cost. The building of motor roads is an excellent example of the second application of labour as it facilitates and cheapens the transport of goods. The German Government decided to introduce a new method of measuring the value of the mark, discarding gold and making the mark represent a labour unit. Taking the total output of labour in the country the number of marks in circulation is limited to that output, and so prices are kept very level, only small fluctuations taking place.

They also proceeded to make a very bold experiment by creating credit through the State to set everyone to work on some useful employment. They were under no delusion as to this fictitious capital. They realised it would have to be replaced by the only real capital, savings from the product of labour, and they took care that every penny was utilised as far as possible to increase the capital wealth of the country. Unfortunately it could not all be utilised for this purpose, because France and Great Britain having refused to consider Hitler's offer to limit standing armies and carry disarmament as far as they were willing to go. People in this country including members of Parliament and newspaper editors are under the delusion that making guns is a legitimate employment of labour and are astonished that the more they spend in this way, the larger the number of unemployed. Making guns makes the country poorer not richer as it is labour misdirected from increasing capital value.

The building of motor roads, the reclamation of land, the improvement of land already under cultivation and forests, the remodelling of factories, the capital expenditure necessary to utilise more fully Germany's raw materials was all useful expenditure increasing the national wealth. When the Nazi Government proceeded by the creation of credit to set everyone to work, the economists here said that inflation and a rise in prices must follow.

No rise in prices took place. This was due in the first place to the centralised control and the willingness of the German people to obey orders, and the fact that no speculative cornering of raw materials and gambling on the stock exchange was allowed, and in the second place to the utilization of the money to produce capital goods of real value. There were no strikes for shorter hours and higher wages. The German workman, knowing that he is not being utilized to pile up huge profits for the capitalists, plays the game. Gradually but steadily this created credit was replaced by real capital, savings obtained from industry.

The interesting result of the calculation of the mark in terms of labour, is that while the other capitalistic countries have millions of unemployed Germany has had to import foreign labour. It is true that most unwillingly she is spending money on munitions owing to the colossal expenditure in munitions here and in France but that is only a fraction of her expenditure which is going to increase the economic strength of Germany.

The mark stands today practically at its value in gold of the old gold mark.

As other countries are busy depreciating their currency, a depreciation which is shown in the rising value of gold, it is necessary to prevent money being taken out of Germany and to make the taking of money out of the country a severely punishable offence. In spite of every care smuggling does go on and there is a market for marks in London where they increase in value as the money of other countries is depreciated more and more.

Germany in trading with other countries is faced by the difficulty that she has no gold, no reserves of foreign exchange and no outside investments the interest on which is paid in goods. She has the further difficulty that she is faced everywhere by high tariffs, quotas and restrictions of output. These restrictions of output and artificial prices for raw materials do not affect us and the U.S.A. who own directly or indirectly most of the world's raw materials which are not owned by France, Holland and Russia.

The English buyer has to pay an artificial price for tin but the owner of the tin mine across the street reaps the advantage. It is money from one English pocket into another English pocket. Germany buys the tin at our artificial price and the same applies to practically all raw materials. She needs colonies especially for semi-tropical products, palm oil, cocoa and so on. It would pay us a thousand times to give back her colonies. The £2,000 millions we are spending on armaments is because we refuse to give them back.

It cost us £8,000 millions to destroy her export trade which existed before the war. How much is it going to cost us to crush her again if we can succeed in doing so?

When trying to develop her export trade Germany could not do it on the plan followed by us with reserves of gold, and foreign exchange, and vast sums from investments abroad, so she applied the same principle that she had applied to her internal economic problem.

She knows the real labour value of her goods in marks, and going to a foreign country she proceeds to barter an exchange of goods for goods which is advantageous to both sides of the bargain. To do this she had obviously to arrange the exchange for a period of several years and give the other country credit to the extent of her immediate purchase of raw materials to be paid in manufactured goods. She has therefore brought trade to its ultimate real basis and cut out the complications of varying currencies.

This is called over here "unfair" method of trading. Every buyer and seller has the right to make such a bargain as suits them both and no one has a right to interfere. Germany is accused of subsidizing exports. This is not peculiar to Germany. We subsidize our coal exports, and this is not a new accusation. It was made after the War and caused Lloyd George to pass the Safeguarding of Industries Act. I believe no action was ever taken under this Act which is still open to anyone who can prove Germany is selling below cost of manufacture.

The real reason for the ferocity of Fleet Street against Germany is that the German Government has determined to work out its own economic problems and avoid international finance like the plague. If Germany came to the City for a loan the financial syndicates that control our "free" press would call off the journalists.

18

The Four Years' Plan

Extraordinary misconceptions of the nature and purpose of the four years' plan have become common in this country.

According to the *Daily Express* our Foreign Office have made it a condition of more friendly relations with Germany that the four years' plan be withdrawn, a most remarkable request as my readers will agree when I have explained what the plan is.

The economic position of Germany, with no gold reserves, heavily indebted abroad and with no colonies and foreign investments, has been dealt with already. Evidently under these circumstances she is thrown entirely on her own resources, and must find what possibilities of development are to be found within her own country.

It is also necessary for her to consider what would happen in case of an attack by the allied powers of Europe. In the last war she was starved out and had in addition a serious shortage of materials required for munitions. She must therefore be prepared for this eventuality.

These considerations are not absent from the councils of other Nations. We are taxing all users of petrol to enable the I.C.I. to make petrol from coal without a loss and are heavily subsidizing agriculture without, it must be admitted, much success.

It is also obvious that increased use of imported raw materials for purposes of manufacture will not do anything to relieve the situation. She must seek to utilize the land to its highest capacity to produce food, and in addition call upon the ingenuity of her chemists to utilize fully her two raw materials - coal and wood.

In order to carry out this task in a comprehensive manner Field Marshall Goering has been appointed as the head of the four years' plan and an organization has been created divided into six offices.

The Board for the production of raw materials has undertaken

a) to increase the production of natural raw materials,

b) the prevention of waste through the use of raw materials for purposes not absolutely necessary,

c) the production of certain synthetic raw materials such as petrol, mineral oils, rubber and artificial wool which are made from coal or wood,

d) the encouragement of relevant research including a complex examination of the German subsoil,

e) the organization and direction of the production of industrial fats.

The section dealing with agriculture has to aim at producing raw materials which are scarce in Germany wherever there is a possibility of agriculture being able to do so.

The cultivation of the Soya bean to obtain a supply of vegetable fats is an excellent example, the production of vegetable fibres and an increase in sheep farming to add to the supply of wool.

It is also the duty of this department to take all possible steps to increase the production of food.

In connection with food an interesting enquiry is to be made into the loss and deterioration of foodstuffs in transit and in the home.

The estimated loss from these two causes is put at 1,500 million marks a year. When we consider how careful and economical the German housewife is, the loss in this country is probably much greater. The savings in this direction involve correct storage of perishable foods and the collection and classification of refuse.

This household refuse is to be used for feeding pigs. Some 4,000 pigs are fed in this way on State property in Magdeburg. A similar arrangement prevails in other cities.

Powers are given in connection with the whole plan for the control of prices.

The difference between the position of Germany before the war and to-day is well illustrated by the following figures. Before the war she had 30,000 million marks invested abroad; to-day she has foreign debts of 13,000 million marks.

Her export trade has now improved sufficiently to show a surplus which is sufficient but no more than sufficient to pay the interest on her foreign debts. The aim of the whole plan is not self-sufficiency, which is both undesirable and impossible, but the making of an economically sound Germany which will lead to a natural development of her export and import trade.

19

The German Colonies

Before the war Germany possessed Tanganyika, Togoland, the Cameroons, Ruanda Urundi, S.W. Africa, Samoa, New Guinea, Nauru, and some small South Sea Islands. As part of the Treaty of Versailles these colonies were all taken from her, and handed over for administration under mandates for the League of Nations. Nothing was settled about their ultimate fate and involved legal discussions have arisen as to whether or not the League can return them to Germany. These discussions are merely obstructive as there can be no question that if we, for instance, asked the League to restore the mandated colonies, the League would do so.

The administration of Tanganyika and Togoland was transferred to Great Britain, Ruanda Urundi to Belgium, S.W. Africa to South Africa, the Cameroons to Great Britain and France, Samoa to New Zealand, Nauru to Australia and the smaller islands to Japan.

In order to queer the pitch, libellous attacks, which have no foundation in fact, have been made on the German administration of these colonies. They have had their Colonial wars with the natives but so have we, and if there is to be a general washing of dirty linen about Africa and digging into past records, no country which has possessions there will be left with a shred of reputation.

Impartial investigators have stated that their administration was efficient and humane, and in fact they were with the usual German thoroughness developing the natural resources of their colonies more rapidly than we do.

Some colonies were captured during the war, others handed over under the Peace Treaty.

President Wilson demanded that a free and open minded and absolutely impartial adjustment of all colonial claims should be made in the Peace Treaty, and it was relying on President Wilson's promise that the German Nation laid down its arms. The reason given for depriving her of all her colonies in the Treaty of Versailles was "the use to which these colonies were put as a base from which to prey on the commerce of the World, and Germany's inability to administer her colonies". The first part of this statement must refer to the fact that the "Emden" made a perfectly legitimate use of the colonies, when engaged in legitimate attacks carried out with the utmost humanity on the commerce of the allies, and the second part of the statement is absurd. Germany was developing her colonial possessions with harbours, roads and railways and laying the foundation for a prosperous future with an organized effort beyond that of other countries.

It has been argued that the total output of the German Colonies for export is so pitiful, amounting to about £6,000,000 a year, that the claim that it will have any real benefit on Germany's financial position is absurd.

There is more than one reply to that. As we have seen Germany's financial policy compelled on her by her foreign debts, and absence of a Gold reserve and large proportion of exports devoted to paying interest, makes it impossible for her to maintain her exchange and yet buy freely abroad. The return of her colonies would enable her to obtain more raw materials within her own system of exchange, and so retrieve her position as a customer in the world's market.

While the gross values are small the actual imports as can be seen by the following [data] cover the whole or a large part of Germany's demand for certain colonial products.

THE CASE FOR GERMANY.

During the time she possessed the colonies she was engaged in development work, which has practically come to a standstill. It is impossible to judge of the final output of produce from these colonies by what was being obtained before the war. The experiment has yet to be tried of testing the capacity for output of these tropical and sub-tropical countries under an active programme and scientific administration and research.

The revolution made by the Dutch in the production of sugar in Java is a case in point. The Dutch, after a prolonged research, have produced a sugar cane suitable for Java with three times the yield of any other sugar cane. We and France have neglected systematic scientific research on the possibilities of our colonies or conducted it on no systematic plan with grossly inadequate funds. We may be sure that this will not be the German policy.

It is obvious from my account of the present monopoly of raw materials that it is impossible to refuse all consideration to Germany with its large growing and vigorous population in one small area in Europe. Far from denying her limited demands for the return of her former colonies, which while assisting her commercially will not give an outlet to her population, we should strive within our vast Empire to give her other opportunities.

We have on the one hand a vast undeveloped Empire, and Germany a vigorous and growing population. If we could persuade our foreign office to cease carping at Germany, there are infinite possibilities between the two nations similar in blood, and closely allied in friendship, for developing the neglected and thinly populated British estate.

Germany has sprung from the war and the terrible Peace with a renewed vigour, strengthened by suffering, and like all vigorous people is increasing in population. We each have qualities which combined can give strength. Let us solve not only European problems but World problems together.

The German colonies produce a wide variety of foodstuffs and raw materials. The exports from Tanganyika in 1935 amounted to £3-4 millions sterling, consisting of coffee, cotton, sisal fibre, peanuts, rice and copra. South West Africa is a cattle country, but has also proved a good breeding ground for karakul sheep supplying the Persian lamb skins. There are also diamond deposits. The exports have therefore fluctuated considerably according to whether demands have been reduced or not. Her total exports in 1935 amounted to £2.5 millions sterling.

Ruanda Urundi exports hides, cotton, coffee and tin ore. £272,000.

The Cameroons produce cacao, palm kernels and palm oil. The total exports amounted in 1935 to £1.3 millions sterling. In the British section the cultivation of bananas on a large scale has rapidly increased owing to the enterprise of Germans who bought back their plantations after the war. In 1935 45,000 tons were exported.

Togo exports cacao, palm oil and palm nuts, and copra, the total exports amounting in 1935 to £490,000.

New Guinea exported copra and gold to the value of £2.3 millions in 1935. Samoa exports copra, the exports for 1935 being £127,000.

The island of Nauru contains many valuable phosphate deposits the export value of which in 1935 was £474,000.

The other small South Sea islands mandated to Japan also produce phosphates and the Japanese have introduced the cultivation of sugar. Total exports of the islands £1.1 million.

The total figure of the exports is not large but the actual amounts exported is in many cases, such as cacao, sufficient to supply the whole German demand. It is not a fair comparison to compare that total with the total of the whole of her export trade.

It must also be remembered that from 1914 to the present time no attempt has been made to develop their territory on scientific lines, and little or nothing done to make roads. The potential wealth of these colonies is enormous if they are developed on a basis of scientific research. This could be done by Germany and judging by past experience will never be done by us. The difference is between Great Britain with such a large garden that most of it grows weeds and it is hardly anywhere cultivated on scientific lines, and Germany with her small allotment to which she will apply intensive cultivation.

It would pay the British Empire to return German East Africa to Germany, as it would become a laboratory providing invaluable data for the cultivation of vast areas in the world with similar climatic conditions.

One of the most curious objections to returning the German colonies, is that all such colonies are a burden and an expense, and more trouble than they were worth. Then why, said Hitler, not allow us to relieve you of these burdens? The reply was strategic reasons, a reply which is meaningless with a German fleet one third the size of ours.

There will probably be difficulties in returning territories mandated to the Dominions, but I suggest as an experiment we return in the meantime German East Africa.

In considering the whole of the area of Africa including the Congo Basin and Tanganyika, it is apt to be forgotten that these vast areas were first under an International Committee in 1885, which still exists and last met in 1919. Among other regulations the region has to offer equal facilities of trade to all Nations. The meeting held in 1919 specially excluded Germany from the privilege but I am told it has never been enforced. Germany ought to be invited to become a member of the Commission and a meeting called to consider the whole question of the future of this area.

20

The Labour Front

To imagine that when we speak of the Trades Unions in Germany before National Socialism we are speaking of organisations which were the same as our Trades Unions in this country, is to misread the whole situation that existed in 1933.

There are three organisations in this country which the wage earning class have built up for themselves, - the Friendly Societies, the Trades Unions and the Co-operative Societies. The Trades Unions, built up through years of struggle when they were illegal institutions, have become part of the recognised organisations of Labour in this country and in some cases a complete scheme for dealing with the problems which arise between Labour and Capital has been developed like that which exists in our railways, with the Trades Unions, the employers organisation and the railway board as final arbiters. It is also necessary to remember that the Trades Unions not only represent the organised workers in labour disputes but are also benefit societies.

There is no necessary connection between Trades Unionism and Socialism. There is no reason why a Trades Union secretary should not be a member of the Primrose League and walk on to the platform of the congress with a primrose in his buttonhole, except that it is one of the things which is not done. To-day he is expected to be a member of the Labour Party and accept without question the pale pink brand of Socialism produced by the Bureaucratic mind, the mere thought of which makes a genuine Communist vomit.

The Socialist resolutions passed every year by the T.U.C. do no harm to anyone, and do not produce the mildest flutter on the Stock Exchange. Every man voting for them is more or less a Capitalist, the Trades Unions themselves have their funds well invested, the Friendly Societies and the Co-operative Societies have hundreds of millions of invested capital. Harcourt once said we are all Socialists now. He might as well have said we are all Capitalists now.

Keir Hardie did the workman a bad turn when he persuaded the Trades Unions to hoist the banner embroidered by the fair hands of Mrs. Webb, but he secured ample funds for the political organisation.

Both the Liberal and the Conservative Parties can claim credit for the advance in social conditions in this country. Only one Party is absolutely sterile and for this reason, that they have adopted a dogma of foreign origin, a patent medicine to cure all social ills, and the Englishman rightly distrusts cure-alls and suspects a neatly logical system because he instinctively distrusts logic outside the Book of Euclid.

The marriage of Trades Unionism to Socialism has been an unfortunate marriage for the workman, but it has not wrecked the Trades Union organisation.

If we now study the Trades Unionism in Germany before 1933, we find the Trades Unions run by political adventurers, entirely absorbed in politics, riddled with Communism, hopelessly in debt, and with an income insufficient to pay the official salaries. It was necessary in the interests of the German workman to sweep away the whole rotten system by which he was being exploited.

It is forgotten that Hitler as a youth and young man lived in great poverty picking up casual labour in Vienna, and he had the inestimable advantage of studying international socialism and communism from the inside, a victim with an intelligent and critical mind. He found out two things in Vienna, - one that the class war leads nowhere, the other that the only people who made money out of the class war were the Jews.

He himself, one of the workers and one of the victims, had long thought out his solution when he ordered his followers to take over the Trades Union organisation, to dismiss the official parasites, and organise in its place the Labour Front, which took over the liabilities of the old Trades Unions and secured for the old members the benefits for which they had paid the money which had been squandered. Quite apart from National Socialism, the Trades Unions were rotten, were bankrupt and something had to be done in the interests of the working man.

The central idea of the Labour Front is an organisation of industry workshop by workshop, in which all those employed in production including the employer and employed are in one organisation with the object of honest production for the good of the German people. Your interests, said Hitler, are not divided, they are the same. While you quarrel over the share of the payment for production, production itself ceases. He determined to replace the economic system of the 19th century, under which labour is bought as a ton of coal is bought and the employer admits no responsibility to the worker, and the State has to intervene at every stage to protect his health and life, by the ideas permeating the old mediaeval guilds. Production was to become human instead of inhuman. We look back with horror upon the exploitation of child labour in the middle of the 19th century.

Karl Marx and Hitler were equally horrified by the inhuman exploitation of the 19th century, but Karl Marx, a journalist, saw it from the outside. Hitler lived and suffered inside the system, and Karl Marx gave the world a message of hate, of spoilation, of a brutal materialism, while Hitler brought it a message of Peace and revival of the message of the gospel. You are all wrong, he cries to the revolutionary Socialists, your way is the way of death. The negative of evil must be driven out by the positive of good. We need an ethical idea with which to permeate the body politic. Lenin in his frenzy used to cry out for torrents of blood. He bathed in them before the end, and the Russian workman has got a new master, the Communist official. "He beat you with whips but I will beat you with scorpions."

Man moves forward by new ethical ideas or rather by the unfolding of the inner meaning of old ideas like the opening of a flower from its green case, petal after petal is displayed and each means a step upwards.

I do not deny that our English Socialism, though I believe it to be wrong on economic lines, is an ethical movement, but Continental Socialism is and has been a very different affair controlled by men lusting for power and exploiting labour for its own ends.

The new organisation of labour is known as the Labour Front, which not only carries on the old benefits of the Trades Unions, and supplies them for half the subscription but has undertaken new activities in the "Strength through Joy" movement which we have never thought of in this country. It has also made universal the payment for holidays, which is based upon the National Socialist idea of the workman as a man with rights as a citizen of the German State, and not merely a penny-in-the-slot machine who is only to be paid when his wheels turn inside. If the T.U.C. instead of passing Socialist resolutions would take up the practical tasks of the Labour Front, they would find universal support in this country and double their membership.

Besides the Labour Front which contains to-day over 20,000,000 members, the National Socialist Government has passed an elaborate Labour Law which I shall make some attempt to describe, but before doing so deal with one of the main accusations against the National Socialist Government, that they have forbidden strikes. Strikes are a form of war, and in the U.S.A. are frequently accompanied by actual warfare, and are destructive and ruinous to both parties and to the community. It took us a long time to recover from the blow to trade of the General Strike. I remember in the Coal Strike of 1921, the Miners Union called out the men at the pumps, thus destroying many millions of pounds of property on which their own living depended. At that time being head of the Technical College in Edinburgh, I wired for our mining students to return from their holidays and go straight to the Fife coal fields and man the pumps. In two days the water was under control, but the Government who had promised to send soldiers to protect the mines were of course not ready, so the mob of miners threw out our boys, the mines were flooded and millions of pounds of property destroyed, and after the strike was over the Fife miners had to wait six months before they could resume their work underground.

I was violently abused by the Fife miners secretary who afterwards became Secretary for Scotland in the Labour Government for taking the side of the mine owners. I replied I have nothing to do with the quarrel between the miners and the mine owners. The mines do not belong either to the mine owners or the miners. They are my property as a member of the British Commonwealth and I have a right to protect my property, a sound National Socialist principle.

It must not be forgotten that while strikes are forbidden lock-outs are also forbidden and it was a lock-out of the miners by the mine owners, before the Commission had reported, that caused the general strike.

If the dreams of the T.U.C. are fulfilled and we become a Socialist State one of the first acts of the State will be to abolish the Trades Unions and forbid strikes.

The Labour Law

The Labour Law is so utterly different from any Act of Parliament in its ideas and expression that it is difficult to follow an intelligible path through its intricate proposals.

In the first place there is the new constitution known as the confidential council in every factory. This body contains representatives from every section of the industry, the workman's representatives being chosen by secret ballot from a list prepared in consultation with the Labour Front, a list for which certain qualifications are necessary such as that to be on the list, a workman must be over 25 and must have belonged to the establishment for a year, with not less than two years' previous experience in a similar industry. The office of a member of the council is an honorary one, and the employer or manager is bound to give the council information necessary for carrying out their duties.

The employer or manager is responsible for the welfare of the workers and the council is to assist the employer in his duties with a view to increase the efficiency of the factory and to deal with any disputes arising between the employer and the employed. The members of the council must all belong to the Labour Front organisation.

The majority of the council may lodge an appeal in writing to the "Labour Front" against any decision of the employer.

The voting list for members is drawn up by the employer and the chairman of the National Socialist cell organisation.

The *"Labour Trustee"* is a government official and appointed to supervise a group of factories; he has no connection with trade or industry.

The duties of the Labour Trustee are as follows: They supervise the formation and operation of the confidential councils and give a decision in case of a dispute. They decide in cases of appeal by the council and may reverse a decision of an employer and issue the necessary ruling themselves.

The Labour Trustee decides respecting proposed dismissals. The employer is bound to give notice in writing of more than 9 dismissals out of a 100 employees, and more than 10% of dismissals over 100. The dismissals cannot take place until four weeks after the Labour Trustee has been notified. Establishment rules of hours and wages and grounds for dismissal without notice must be issued in writing by the employer to the work people.

The Labour Trustees may lay down guiding principles for each establishment and rules and general rates where minimum conditions of employment are needed, for the protection of the work people. The Labour Trustee has great powers over his district and can make rules to apply to the special conditions of that district. The Labour Trustee appoints an advisory council of experts for the various branches of industry in his district for consultation on questions which are of a general nature or which involve a principle. Three fourths of the experts must be chosen from lists of individuals drawn up by the Labour Front.

Employers and members of the confidential councils shall be selected in equal numbers. One fourth of the members can be appointed by the Labour Trustee from suitable persons in the district. The Labour Trustee can appoint a committee of experts to advise in individual cases.

The Labour Courts

If an employee is dismissed after one year's employment in an establishment of not less than ten persons he may lodge a complaint with the Labour Court. The complaint must be accompanied by a report from the confidential council that the continuance of employment has been unsuccessfully raised by them.

If the Court decides the reversal of the dismissal it shall include in the sentence an amount of compensation if the employer refuses to revoke the dismissal. It will be noted that the employee is carefully guarded from wrongful dismissal. He has first an appeal to his own confidential council and then to the Labour Court.

Social Honour Courts

One of the most interesting ideas in the Labour Law is the Social Honour Court.

The idea of the Social Honour Court is that a person can harm the State by actions which are not illegal and that the employers and employees in a working community have responsibilities to each other, the works and the State. Offences under this category are as follows:

- If an employer exploits his workmen, or abuses his authority, or is disobedient to instructions given by the Labour Trustee.
- If a member of the confidential council reveals without authority confidential information or technical or business secrets which have become known to him through his duties as a member of the confidential council.
- If an employee endangers industrial peace by maliciously provoking other employees, or
- if a confidential man interferes unduly in the conduct of the establishment, or continually disturbs the community spirit.

The Honour Court consists of an official of the judiciary appointed by the Federal Minister of Justice and the Federal Minister of Labour, as chairman, one leader of an establishment and one confidential man as assessors. These two are selected by the chairman from a list drawn up by the German Labour Front.

The Honour Courts may impose a warning, a reprimand, a disciplinary fine, disqualification for the position of leader, or confidential man, and removal of the offender from his post.

Decisions on offences against social honour are given on the application of the Labour Trustee by an Honour Court established for each Labour Trustee's district.

Strength Through Joy

There must have been a time before the black cloud of industrialisation pouring from a million factory chimneys destroyed joy in life, when the people however poor they may have been had some communal pleasures. The folk songs, the peasant dancing, the beautiful peasant costumes worn on important occasions all indicate that such a time once existed.

The beauty of the buildings in our villages also show a people living in the land who had the capacity for appreciating and the pleasure in building the house and the Church. Mankind does not live by bread alone and this is the central idea of the "Strength through Joy" organisation which is a branch of the Labour Front.

The movement has taken four directions. One is that the pleasures of the theatre, the concert hall, and travel, even as far as Madeira, could be put in the reach of all at a very small expenditure by the individual. Last year by means of the "Strength through Joy" organisation 4,850,000 German work people attended theatres. Travelling companies that go from village to village have been organised, the theatres have agreed to give certain special performances at cheap prices, the whole movement has not only brought the theatre to every door but has proved profitable for the theatres themselves.

Excellent music is now also available and the German has always had a love for good music.

The organisation of travel during holidays at first confined to Germany is now being extended overseas and the organisation is now building its own ships for holiday excursions. Last year eleven million workers enjoyed travel in Germany and abroad through the organisation.

The second side of their organisation is the development of music and dramatic societies and athletic clubs. All this of course would have been impossible by a central organisation. The fact is the "Strength through Joy" idea has caught on in Germany, and with a little guidance from headquarters the villages and the workshops are organising these things for themselves. Broadcasting is being used to transmit the best of their local efforts.

The third idea is improving factory conditions, not only by providing washing and bathing facilities and dining rooms, but by making the factories inside more pleasant places, and turning waste ground outside into gardens, and even converting the hideous dumps into things pleasant to look at. Factories in this country are often pleasant places and well equipped. Bryant and Mays in East London is surrounded by gardens and tennis grounds for their employees. But it is only necessary to penetrate the industrial quarters of Manchester, of the Five Towns, of Birmingham, or of Glasgow, to realise their appallingly dreary ugliness.

50,000,000 marks have been spent on improving the factories since the "Strength through Joy" movement was started, and prizes are given for the most beautiful villages.

The fourth side is their very complete organisation of educational work.

The astounding success of this movement would never have been achieved, as I have said, by a central organisation alone. The people of Germany have grasped the idea of National Socialism and with a little direction and suggestions from headquarters are working out the practical application for themselves. Hitler is right when he says, "I represent today the German people more closely than any Prime Minister of a Democratic country". The lightest touch on the wheel from the captain is all that is needed to steer the ship.

21

Agriculture

I have already dealt briefly in the chapter on Economics with the agricultural problem, but it is so important, being the foundation on which everything rests, that I propose to discuss it here in more detail. It is also of interest as showing the way in which the National Socialist Government approaches an economic problem. They begin by approaching it as a social problem, the well-being of the agriculturist and his family and their recognition as a living and essential part of the community being the first question to be considered. In no case do they indulge in revolutionary economics. They have not only accepted the existing economic structure in Germany, but they go further than that and search into the past history to find a solid foundation on which to build. Germany has her big land owners but she also has her peasant proprietors amounting to more than 500,000 families among whom the custom of inheritance from father to son is very largely prevalent.

The *Bauer*, the Peasant Proprietor is the solid foundation, Hitler says, on which to build a state, and he must be established and protected by law so as to form a Peasant Aristocracy, proud of their position in the commonwealth and recognition by the State. It is a class alas absent in this country except where a county council has established small holdings. The English yeoman and peasant farmer was destroyed by the robbery of the commons and the enclosure act.

THE CASE FOR GERMANY.

In France, in Germany and in Austria, the farm house of the peasant is familiar in the landscape, sometimes clustered in villages, in other places far apart. Under one roof is the family house, and storage for hay, and room for all the pigs and cattle during the hard continental winter, when everything must be gathered under one roof. The peasant is an interesting feature of most continental countries. In Italy he scorns to marry a townsman and it is among them that you find purity of race and handsome men and beautiful girls. The castle on the mountain side has long been a ruin. The peasant's home continues from one generation to another.

In Spain the population of the cities have no national characteristics or race features, and are poor undergrown specimens of humanity. I have never forgotten seeing the peasants riding into Toledo in their picturesque costumes. These were the men who had conquered Mexico and Peru and showed race in every feature.

Hitler is right, therefore, when he builds the German State on the peasant, a race which we destroyed in the 18th century to satisfy the greed of our land owners.

While in Russia the Soviet have been striving to destroy the peasant and convert him into a communal wage slave, a struggle in which millions have died of starvation, Hitler has built his State on the peasant as its foundation.

The contrast between Communism and National Socialism could not be more marked. The National Socialist builds on a long tried system of land ownership; Communism sweeps it all away in the name of an untried economic theory. Under the law establishing the peasant it has been made illegal to lend money on the security of the house and land and they cannot be sold in payment of debts.

Another interesting provision is that any destitute member of the family has the right to claim the shelter of the ancestral home.

We shall never solve our agricultural difficulties in this country until the man who tills the soil owns the soil or has it in perpetual lease direct from the State.

Another important principle established in Germany is that the land yields its best return to the intense cultivation of the small unit of land. The application of mass production ideas to the land has already in the U.S.A. and in Australia converted millions of acres into a desert. The small economic unit is the right principle for cultivation but it is at a disadvantage in selling the product, and this is where the second part of the organisation comes in.

On the 13th September, 1933, the German Government enacted as the basic law for agriculture, the National Food Corporation Act which decided the provisional constitution of this organisation. Thus the Corporation was lifted from the level of a voluntary organisation to the position of a public body.

The National Food Corporation became a compulsory institution for the persons affected, and is subject to official supervision. Therefore the National Food Corporation includes not only the productive group - that is agriculture itself - but also all those groups which are in any way concerned with providing the German nation with food. They comprise the groups engaged in the manufacture of various commodities out of these products as well as those concerned with the distribution to the consumer. By reason of this co-operation, the National Food Corporation forms a body consisting of producers, manufacturers and distributors all of whom are of equal importance within this organisation.

The following is a rough outline of the organisation of the National Food Corporation. At the head of the whole organisation of the National Food Corporation is the National Peasants Führer R. Walther Darré with his deputy.

To assist him the Peasants Führer has an advisory body, the *Reichsbauernrat* (National Peasants Council), membership of which is purely honorary. Its members are nominated by the Peasants Führer.

In the *Stabsamt* (Planning Dept.) the Peasants Führer has created an institution where the work is planned for many years ahead by several main sections which deal with questions of trade and industry, law, comparative agriculture, training in agricultural practice and theory, the introduction of up-to-date working methods, peasant customs and racial matters.

In the *Verwaltungsamt* (Executive Department) the plans already decided on by the Stabsamt are put into operation.

Section I of the *Verwaltungsamt* is concerned with the welfare of the individual, be he the owner of an agricultural estate, that is to say peasant or agriculturist, tenant farmer or agricultural labourer. All questions bearing on the rural population are treated here.

Section II of the *Verwaltungsamt* deals with all questions of rural economy, with the homestead, with the estate, in short with everything connected with the peasant's calling. It comprises, besides the technical side, all matters connected with soil, crops, and plant life, training, forestry, agricultural implements and machinery as well as with domestic economy.

Section III of the *Verwaltungsamt* is responsible for the organisation of the market, e.g. for questions of the distribution of supplies for the utilization or processing of agricultural produce. The economic bodies concerned are grouped in eighteen associations which - under their own administration - have been assigned special duties to the community but are under the direction of Section III. The following are the most important organisations:

Hauptvereinigung der Deutschen Getreidewirtschaft.
National Union of Corn *[Scriptorium: actually, Grain]* Producers and Distributors).

Hauptvereinigung der Deutschen Viehwirtschaft.
(National Union of Live-stock Breeders and Dealers).

Hauptvereinigung der Deutschen Milchwirtschaft.
(National Union of Milk Producers and Distributors).

Hauptvereinigung der Deutschen Eierwirtschaft.
(National Union of Egg Producers and Distributors).

Hauptvereinigung der Deutschen Gartenbauwirtschaft.
(National Union of Market Gardeners).

Reichsverband Deutscher landwirtschaftlicher Genossenschaften.
(National Union of German Agricultural Co-operative Societies).

Hauptvereinigung der Deutschen Brauwirtschaft.
(National Union of the German Brewing Industry).

Wirtschaftliche Vereinigung der Deutschen Süsswarenwirtschaft.
(Economical Union of Confectioneries).

Hauptvereinigung der Deutschen Fischwirtschaft.
(National Union of the Fishing Trade).

Wirtschaftliche Vereinigung der Margarine- und Kunstspeisefettindustrie.
(Union of the Margarine and Artificial Fat Industry).

Hauptvereinigung der Deutschen Kartoffelwirtschaft.
(National Union of Potato Growers and Distributors).

In addition to the sections enumerated, the *Verwaltungsamt* has three more sections. Two of these are concerned with financial matters and questions of personnel while the section "Public Enlightenment" is responsible for the press, broadcasting, the organisation of exhibitions, films, lectures, agricultural market information, advertising, literature, publishing, archives, and libraries.

An Inspector-General has been appointed to superintend the setting into operation of special schemes and to control the offices of the *Landes- und Kreisbauernschaften* (Regional and District Peasant Associations).

The National Food Corporation is subdivided into *Landesbauernschaften* (Regional Peasant Associations) whose area generally coincides with that of the various German Federal States or the Prussian provinces. The *Landesbauernführer* (Regional Peasants Führer) and his deputy are responsible for the work of the Regional Associations. The organisation is similar to that of the *Verwaltungsamt* for the whole of the Reich, though on a smaller scale. There are in all twenty Regional Associations which are in turn subdivided into *Kreis-* and *Ortsbauernschaften* (District and Local Peasant Associations).

The Districts Association are, in the main, in close touch with the peasants and land owners and supply them with such advice as cannot be supplied by the Local Associations.

Each District Association is headed by a District Association Führer who holds an honorary position.

The administration of the Local Associations is also an honorary function. The Führer of the Local Association is in uninterrupted touch with each peasant and thus holds a particularly responsible office.

Finally, it should be mentioned that the National Food Corporation also supervises the peasants' schools, the agricultural schools and colleges, and the stock breeding boards, so that it includes in its sphere of activity everything connected with the task for which it is competent.

Marketing regulations

It has already been intimated that the National Socialist agrarian policy has abandoned (in the case of particularly important food products) the capitalistic maxim that the price is dependent on supply and demand. In this way not only the distributors and manufacturers but also the producers of our food supplies are no longer forced to go in for financial speculation. In this respect, the poorer classes were at the greatest disadvantage; for, lacking the necessary capital to await favourable times, they had to sell their goods prematurely in order to obtain ready money. The peasant, as a rule, belonged to the class of speculators with limited capital, for he can generally turn over his capital only once a year. The same applied to the middle-sized industries immediately connected with agricultural produce, such as flour mills and breweries. As a result, many of the small and middle-sized concerns were taken over by larger firms with considerable capital, a development unfavourable to national economy. The harmful influence of this speculation was counteracted by the marketing regulations laid down by the National Socialist agrarian policy which introduced fixed prices, and fixed prices means fair prices.

A fair price must fulfil the double condition of protecting both the producer and the consumer. The peasant and the agriculturist must be protected against the necessity of having to sell their products at cut prices if they are to sell them at all; whereas the consumer's interests must be guarded against being robbed at times when, owing to seasonal changes, production falls off. The fixed price should be high enough to cover the cost of production and to guarantee the proper continuance of agricultural work. On the other hand, it must be low enough to exclude the possibility of the consumer's being robbed; the consumer, in fact, should always be able to rely on stable prices which are in proportion to his income. In this way the prices of bread, milk and butter, for example, have remained stationary for years, though, from a speculative point of view, price fluctuations would have been technically justified by the variation in the yield of the annual crops etc. The fixing of the prices has, however, prevented this to the benefit of both parties. With regard to the necessities of daily life, the prices have also been fixed, generally speaking, for the dealers' trade as well as for the trader utilizing or processing agricultural produce. In fixing the rate of the middleman's margin it was not intended to kill this trade since it has long shown its value as a machinery for private distribution. The idea was simply to

THE CASE FOR GERMANY.

remove any possibility of financial speculation on the part of anyone concerned.

But the marketing regulations have other important functions apart from mere price regulation. In the first place they regulate the functioning of the entire system of manufacture and distribution. Furthermore, by means of the marketing regulations a systematic organisation of the sale of agricultural products is secured. This shall hereunder be demonstrated by an example taken from the dairy business.

Before the agricultural marketing regulations were introduced, the milk market was in a chaotic state. Obviously, everyone wished to share in supplying milk to the big towns, because the best prices were to be obtained there. The milk supplied to Berlin, for instance, did not all come from the surrounding districts, but was in part sent hundreds of miles, even from the Allgäu, a district situated in the extreme south of Germany. This is explained by the fact that the Allgäu peasant received locally for his home made butter and cheese such a poor return that he found it a better paying proposition to send his milk to Berlin, in spite of the distance. Apart from the middleman's profit there was the enormous cost of haulage over some 435 miles to be paid. Things went from bad to worse, and no solution appeared possible. At the same time it was found impossible to lower the retail price because the unproductive middleman's charges prevented any reduction. When marketing regulations were introduced, the dairy business throughout Germany was divided into certain milk supply regions, an arrangement which has proved extremely beneficial to the entire dairy trade.

Similar arrangements have been made for the supply of other commodities.

The marketing regulations also endeavour to improve the quality of all products of German soil. The price of superior qualities cannot be demanded for inferior qualities; the idea of improving the quality is therefore not penalized but encouraged. For purposes of research in the direction of the improvement of quality the National Food Corporation is provided with all manner of research and teaching institutions. Hence marketing regulations imply not stagnation but increased efficiency.

Where necessary, the marketing regulations also help to secure order and discipline in the market. The problem of food supplies cannot be allowed to depend on the arbitrary action of individuals to the extent of affecting the common interest. The private individual's initiative is in no way restricted, but competition must be kept within bounds, so as not to become harmful to the national economy. In cases of harmful and unnecessary competition the National Food Corporation can take decisive action by licensing only such a number of businesses in any locality or districts as may be reasonably expected to make a living. It may be pointed out once more that marketing regulations are not identical with "planned economy". Nobody intends to limit the area under the plough or to enforce certain rules concerning cultivation. There is a fundamental difference between marketing regulations and "planned economy".

To sum up, the following are the functions assigned to the marketing regulations:

I. Protection of the producer.
>Fair, fixed prices.
>Assured sales.

II. Protection of the consumer.
>Fair and stable prices for the consumer.
>Fair supply even in case of scarcity.
>Guaranty of quality.
>Control of supplies.

III. Organised movement of goods, organised manufacture.
>Compulsory Pools *(Andienungspflicht)*.
>Sensible distribution of goods.
>Fixing of quotas.
>Fixing of a fair margin of profit.
>Principle of efficiency.

THE CASE FOR GERMANY.

Establishing a New German Peasantry

The term *ländliche Siedlung* (rural settlement) is more generally used than *Neubildung Deutschen Bauerntums* (Establishing a New German Peasantry); the latter, however, gives a clearer idea of the actual facts. Miniature and suburban settlements will not be considered here, nor for that matter cottage settlements which, from small beginnings, develop into peasant holdings.

It is the aim of the National Food Corporation to create as many new peasants' estates as possible, particularly in thinly populated districts. They must have the size of at least one *Ackernahrung* (i.e. sustaining a man, his wife and two children), thus guaranteeing a livelihood from the soil worked.

The success hitherto attained in establishing a new German peasantry is, strange to say, hard to express in figures. Thus, not much is gained by stating that, in 1934, nearly 5,000 new estates were set up. Neither can a clear idea of the development in this direction be gathered from the fact that 144,617 hectares (approximately 357,000 acres) of land in all parts of Germany were provided for purposes of internal colonisation in 1934. But in comparison with the fact that, during the years 1919 to 1932, on the average only 67,184 hectares (approximately 165,000 acres) per year were provided for the same purpose, it will easily be seen that the establishment of new peasants' estates is proceeding rapidly.

There are three ways for providing land for this purpose.

A certain acreage will be provided out of the large landed estates. It should, however, be made clear that this does not mean any compulsory expropriation of large properties, but that the owners will be compensated for the land acquired for this purpose. Besides privately owned land, government property also will be utilized for internal colonization, as far as technical conditions permit. The *Reichssiedlungsgesetz* (Reich Act to make provision for Internal Colonization) provides the possibility of obtaining from private and public estates in the manner described an acreage of nearly 1.7 million hectares (approximately 4.2 million acres) with a view to creating new agricultural land. It is, however, not yet possible to say when the whole of this land will be available.

A second possibility of providing land for agricultural purposes is the cultivation of waste land, bogs, fens and swamps. This method of obtaining arable soil is particularly important since in this way useless land is turned into useful land. In contrast to the cultivation of bogs we cannot base exaggerated hopes on the cultivation of waste land, because there is only a limited quantity of the latter available. It must also be borne in mind that certain stretches of waste land can never be made productive owing to peculiarities of conditions such as climate, altitude, nature of the soil, etc., which cannot very well be changed. The total area in Germany utilisable from an agrarian point of view is about 30 million hectares (approximately 73 million acres). It would be unlike the German peasant to have allowed millions of hectares of waste land to lie idle beside his good fields. In the case of bogs and swamps, the conditions, as already pointed out, are entirely different. Here, in contrast to the case of waste land, the individual has generally no possibility of undertaking by himself any successful and comprehensive reclamation. Results can only be realised when a large part or the entire area of the bog is tackled at the same time. For this reason it has been advisable to make use of the *Arbeitsdienst* (Labour Service) for the cultivation of waste land. We may estimate the area of bog and waste land capable of being cultivated at about 2 million hectares (approximately 5 million acres). It is, of course, impossible to achieve great results at short notice. Nevertheless, extensive reclamation of bog and waste land, amounting to over 200,000 hectares (approximately 500,000 acres) has already begun. This land is situated in all parts of Germany. The most important reclamation would appear to be the Rhin and Havel swamps near Berlin, the Sprotte fens in Silesia, the Ried marshes in Hesse, the Chiemgau bog and the Danube marshes in Bavaria and the swamps on the left bank of the river Ems in North West Germany. In the Labour

Service young Germans of all classes have an opportunity of becoming acquainted with and acquiring respect for the work involved in the reclamation of the German bogs and marshes.

Unfailing energy and tenacity have been and will be called for in order to make use of this possibility of obtaining new land, namely by reclamation from the sea. Extensive dykes are required. Since the German nation, the "People without Space", needs new land, they will not shrink even from the most difficult tasks. Within a 50-year programme, the North Sea on the West coast of Schleswig-Holstein alone is to yield up 100,000 hectares (approximately 250,000 acres) of new land. Good results have already been obtained. In 1935 the Adolf Hitler polder, 1,334 hectares (approximately 3,300 acres) in area, and the Hermann Göring polder, 550 hectares (approximately 1,300 acres) in area, were inaugurated. In this way land for nearly one hundred peasant estates under the new Act has been provided. A considerably greater number of handcraftsmen's settlements have also been formed here.

The selection of new peasants depends on certain conditions. It goes without saying that they must be of German descent. The peasant and his wife must be valuable individuals from a racial point of view and come from healthy stock, so that a guaranty is provided for healthy offspring. Families with many children are given preference when new land is being distributed. It is also of primary importance that the applicant should be able to prove that he himself as well as his family are suited to the life. These new peasant estates must not be regarded as a practising ground for all and anyone to try their hands at experimenting, nor as an instructional institution for those who consider themselves fitted for agricultural work. Technical qualifications are therefore required under all circumstances. Only where these primary conditions are satisfied the financial situation of the applicant is considered. For financing these undertakings definite rules have been drawn up on lines which make it possible even for persons of moderate means to take over one of those new estates.

The establishment of these new peasant estates is undertaken by estate companies under the supervision of competent authorities, an arrangement which guarantees close co-operation with the National Food Corporation. The new agricultural estates are got ready up to a point from which it is possible to begin to work them properly whereafter every peasant is free to make the best use possible of the opportunity afforded him for improving his position according to his personal energy and for endeavouring to do his best for his own welfare and that of his descendants. Only by struggling to succeed will he become attached to the soil. Not only younger sons of peasants are to be provided with a new estate, but everyone capable of fulfilling the required conditions, particularly agricultural labourers. Since these latter cannot, as a rule, compete with the others financially, especially favourable conditions will apply in their case, and they will thus be provided with the possibility of rising in the social scale.

Besides these fundamental matters a certain number of other points have to be considered in connection with the planning of houses, schools, and with similar questions. Their solution will, as a rule, be arrived at in practice. As a result of the close co-operation between the competent authorities, the National Food Corporation and the estate companies, the conditions laid down by the National Food Corporation will always be carefully observed.

This great work of settlement and internal colonization going on in Germany serves the end of national reconstruction. **Where reconstruction is taking place, peace must prevail. Hence Germany too needs peace for her work.**

22

Munich and After

*"Why do the heathens rage
and the people imagine a vain thing?"*

Since the signing of the Peace Pact between Chamberlain and Hitler in September events have moved rapidly in Europe. The reply in Great Britain to the Peace Pact was a violent campaign in the British Press against Germany, and an attack on Chamberlain's policy both by the Opposition in Parliament and by many members of his own party. The Peace Pact was ignored and war with Germany discussed as a matter of course. Chamberlain was only able to save his position by increasing enormously the expenditure on armaments.

The large number of people in this country who believe a good understanding with Germany essential had no opportunity of putting forward their point of view in the press. The members of Parliament were intimidated by the press campaign. The only institution left where a free expression of opinion was possible was the House of Lords. The warmongers controlled both the press and the B.B.C.

The final victory of Franco enormously strengthened the position of the Axis in Europe to the great astonishment of our press who, having pursued him with a vile campaign of calumny during the war, assisted by a political agitation in this country, imagined that he would join with us. Franco's reply to our advances was to join the anti-Comintern Pact and France, who had taken the side of the Communists, found herself with three potential enemies on her three frontiers.

Hungary also joined the anti-Comintern Pact, and Jugoslavia entered into the closest friendship with Germany and Italy, so that Great Britain and France found themselves faced with a formidable bloc in Europe, of nations they had treated with hostility or indifference.

President Roosevelt next joined the campaign against Germany and Italy. The Press and the wireless had been used for months to spread lies about Germany and when the ground had been prepared Roosevelt made a violent attack on Germany and Italy, and proposed a combination of the Democracies against them and a trade boycott. As Senator Pittman put it clearly, *"Why kill them when we can starve them?"*

These proposals by Roosevelt were acclaimed by our Press but it soon became evident that the people in the U.S.A. were not going to be drawn into another European war and that Roosevelt would find it very difficult to get the Neutrality Law altered so that he could if he chose supply munitions to one side and not to the other, thus putting into the hands of the President the decision of Peace or War.

It was obvious that Germany and Italy could not continue to ignore the feverish preparations for war in Great Britain, France and the U.S.A., and consequently two dramatic events took place, one quickly following on the other.

Slovakia separated herself from Czechoslovakia, claiming independence. The Czech Government, faced by internal revolution, asked Germany to intervene and Germany occupied Bohemia and Moravia, incorporating them as a Protectorate in the Reich. It was impossible any longer to tolerate this promontory penetrating deep into Germany and governed by people who were largely communistic and hostile to Germany, an area which French military authorities had openly stated would be used as a base for bombing planes, aiming at destroying the cities of Germany.

It was evident from the replies made by Mr. Chamberlain and Lord Halifax that they did not regard the occupation of Bohemia and

THE CASE FOR GERMANY.

Moravia as a matter affecting our interests, as, owing to the break-away of Slovakia, **Czechoslovakia had ceased to exist and an occupation by German troops made at the request of the Czech Government could hardly be described as an act of military aggression.**

Then the storm cloud, organised by those working for war, burst and has swept the Government like helpless logs in its torrent towards war. The public excitement was increased by the publication in the London Press of a message purporting to come from Rumania - but now believed to have been concocted in London - to the effect that Germany had threatened Rumania with war if she did not give her a complete monopoly of all her external trade. The British Ambassador in Berlin was instructed to lodge a protest with the German Government, and to tear up the Peace Pact signed by Herr Hitler and Mr. Chamberlain.

This was followed later by the occupation of Albania by Italy thus securing the Adriatic from the hostile fleets of England and France bombarding Italian towns.

According to Mr. Chamberlain these two necessary acts of self defence filled the whole world with "horror". I have been young and now am old and in my lifetime I have seen Great Britain wage war after war to "extend" the Empire. It is not for us, satiated with conquest, and oppressing today by force the Arabs in Palestine - a country in which we are interlopers, and which incidentally occupies a strategic position on the Mediterranean, - to criticise the actions of other nations.

These two inevitable acts were received quite calmly in Europe but were made the excuse for a fresh campaign here and in the States in which it was stated that Germany and Italy meant to invade and annex all the small nations in Europe as a preliminary to world conquest, and our Press arranged for alarmist messages from every capital in Europe. An imaginary crisis was created and the enemies of Chamberlain gathered their forces to turn him out of office. Churchill, Eden and their friends worked night and day to organise a revolt in the Conservative Party, and Fleet Street said he would not remain in power for another week. If he fell, Eden, who cannot speak without showing his insolent attitude to the German people, Churchill, and their friends would form a government.

Chamberlain saved himself by his speech in Birmingham attacking Hitler, and by proposing to resuscitate the old plan which he had only a year ago condemned as unworkable - a coalition of the small nations in Europe against Germany. Without waiting to be asked, we promised Poland to defend her if Germany attacked her independence, went round Europe trying to draw the small nations into a combination against Germany, and approached the Soviet for the same purpose. When Italy occupied Albania, we hastened to offer Greece and Albania our defence if their independence was attacked. The response to these efforts has been very remarkable. Ten nations, in addition to France and Italy, are in contact with the German frontier. Of these Belgium is guaranteed by England, France and Germany. Of the other nine, only Poland has accepted. The other eight have declined our offer of protection, saying they have no cause for alarm, and in addition, Norway, Sweden, Finland, Latvia, Estonia and Bulgaria stand aloof. A Norwegian Minister speaking the other day declared that for three hundred years, the Scandinavian countries have been fighting with England for the right to maintain their neutrality. Rumania and Greece have thanked us for our offer to defend them, but have explained that they have no intention of entering into a reciprocal treaty and only Portugal, Poland and Turkey have agreed to a mutually defensive treaty. Rumania has been rewarded with a loan of five million pounds, for graciously allowing us to defend her. The Soviet in spite of our beseeching attitude has so far not come to any agreement with us. The part they will play if war should come, is that of the jackal feasting on the corpses of the slain.

All we have done is to present Hitler with a splendid testimonial from the small nations in Europe.

Just as we were forced by the "City" to crush the small independent Boer Republic in order to gain control of the gold mines, so the real reason, why we are interfering in Poland, Rumania and Greece, is that our financiers have large interests in the Polish coal mines where the

THE CASE FOR GERMANY.

miners' wages are disgracefully low, Rumanian oil and Greek banking. A pipe line runs from the oil fields of poverty stricken Rumania to the city of London, pouring the wealth of that country into the pockets of our financiers. They are determined that Germany be warned off these countries, where they have established a monopoly of financial control. The British public are deceived by the cry "Defend the independence of small nations".

The attempt we are making to persuade the Soviet to invade Europe, pouring in hordes of barbaric troops from European and Asiatic Russia, whose advance would be accompanied by Communist risings and massacres, is probably the greatest crime against Christianity and civilization in the history of Europe.

By following this extraordinary foreign policy our Government has sinned against four principles which should govern the foreign policy of nations.

No Government has the right to pledge the lives of the people, except in self defence or defence of a vital interest. The inclusion of Bohemia in the Reich touches no interest of ours.

No Government has a right to hand the control of its foreign policy to another nation or nations. Let us suppose, for instance, that Greece quarrelled with Italy and they went to war; we are bound to fight for Greece whether she is right or wrong.

The following quotation from a speech made by Captain Euan Wallace, Minister of Transport, at Bognor, condemns the government foreign policy out of their own mouths.

> "Let us make no mistake about it, the decision whether we will fight has been taken out of the hands of the people of this country, and out of the hands of our governors. We have made commitments which are automatic. If those commitments are broken, this country is committed for better or for worse to take up arms."

It is the duty of a Government to reduce outside commitments which may lead to war, and to secure the friendship of all nations. Our Government has increased our commitments which may lead to war, and by this action caused the Peace Pact and the Naval Treaty with Germany to be torn up. We had torn up the Peace Pact and Germany has now quite reasonably denounced the Naval Pact which was of great value to us. The final result of our action has been that Hitler is freed from his Peace Treaty with Poland and any restraint in strengthening his navy, so that he is left with a distinct diplomatic gain by our action.

No Government has the right to lure a nation into war with a third nation if they cannot fulfil their offers of help. If Poland, having accepted our advances, makes war on Germany, we could not by any possibility go to her assistance.

As the Führer pointed out in his speech on April 28, 1939, when he first signed a Peace Pact with Poland he made no objections to the existing "Mutual Security Treaty" with France; but for Poland, having signed the Peace Pact, to make a treaty with Great Britain undertaking to make war on Germany under certain conditions, is an obvious breach of the Peace Pact.

What does Poland imagine she gains by this move? The Polish Corridor is an injustice to Germany and many people are astonished that she has put up with it so long. Danzig is as much a German city as Liverpool is English. Suppose we had lost the War and Germany had given Liverpool to De Valera? How long would we have tolerated that state of affairs?

Hitler made the Peace Pact with Poland and has faithfully observed it. Now they have broken it he is free to take back the Polish Corridor and include Danzig in the Reich. If Poland imagines that she can drag England into a war with Germany about Danzig she is greatly mistaken. Our Government has been careful to guard themselves on that point. Supposing Poland declares war and does manage to bring us in it will not save her. We are as helpless to save her as if she was on the Planet

Mars. For us to tempt her to make such a suicidal war is an act of mischief deliberately disturbing the Peace of Europe.

Roosevelt who hopes for a third term of office in spite of having landed the U.S.A. with a huge internal debt and 20 millions people on the dole, was looking out for a good slogan and thought that a call to the Democracies to defend "Christianity, Democracy and International Good Faith" would do.

He has had to retreat, and has thrown out a smoke screen to hide his retreat by sending to the World Press and Hitler and Mussolini an absurd document, in which they are told to pledge themselves to Peace for 25 years with a long list of nations, and then hand their future over to a world congress controlled by the three Democracies who were responsible for the Treaty of Versailles. This has been hailed as a wonderful document by the Governments of Great Britain and France.

In the meantime Peace among the nations of the Danube Basin and of the Balkans is being assured by Hitler and Mussolini, who are having conference with the various Prime Ministers and Foreign Secretaries. There are three dangers to Peace, the territorial demands of Hungary and of Bulgaria, and the trouble with the Croatians, but with the friendly assistance of Germany and Italy both nations will doubtless be able to come to terms with their neighbours.

These nations are all centering round the Axis because it will give them the three things which the people of Europe most desire, - Peace, ordered stable Government, and trade.

The Totalitarian States stand for certain fundamental principles:
- Peace among the nations, each following out its own economic life.
- Government with only one object - the good of the people, instead of being used for the struggle for power of rival political Parties.
- The abolition of Politicians.
- The abolition of the use of the Press controlled by financial groups to promote war by spreading lies.

- A higher conception of the relation of the individual to the community, which is not merely negative - the obeying of the law - but positive, - the service of the community being the first duty.
- A stable economic and financial system and work for all.
- Freedom from control by international finance.
- Arms for defence but not for attack.

It is obvious that the European nations are grouping themselves in friendly alliance round the Axis and it is time we recognised that fact and accepted the friendship which has been offered us by Germany and Italy.

It is also time that France, for long under the influence of our foreign office with its pernicious traditions, reversed her policy and made friends with her neighbours who have no quarrel with her, settled the quite reasonable demands of Italy, and developed trade with the three countries on her frontiers.

Why should France sacrifice so much because we choose to quarrel with Germany?

There will probably be no war in Europe because Hitler and Mussolini stand for Peace.

The Europeans are settling down to a long Peace, which clears the deck for the larger question of World Trade and the huge monopoly of Gold, Raw materials and tropical and sub-tropical products held by the three Democracies and the Soviet.

In every speech Hitler and Mussolini have given warning on this matter and they not only represent the needs of themselves and Japan but many other nations.

This of course is what Roosevelt is really thinking about. He is prepared to plunge into a World War to defend Monopoly in the name of "Christianity, Democracy and Good Faith."

The power of the Monopolists is colossal. They possess the world's wealth, rule a great part of the world's population, and have at their command our overwhelming sea power, which enables them to control

THE CASE FOR GERMANY.

trade on the high seas, and as we have seen, Roosevelt has already proposed that a trade boycott force the Have Nots into submission.

It is really for this reason that Germany is seeking to develop trade on the old trade route from Asia to Europe and it is for this reason that we are trying to prevent it.

While in Parliament the Government talk about small nationalities, the Conservative Party organisation through its political instructors is telling us that we do not care what happens to small nationalities, but we must stop the development of Germany's trade in the Danube Basin and the Balkans so as to be able to starve her out by a blockade. It is obviously not only in the interest of the Have Nots, but of the whole world and even of the Monopolists themselves that the trade of the world be set free. Strangely enough the Monopolists are suffering most from their own policy having huge armies of unemployed.

The British Empire when it was a Free Trade Empire had the goodwill of all the world. To-day when it has surrounded itself with tariffs, Ottawa agreements, quotas and international restrictions on output, it no longer has that goodwill which was its real strength, and piling armaments on armaments is not the solution of the question.

Not so important but of great interest is the Gold monopoly, a monopoly not only of the Gold available but the world's Gold mines which the Monopolists share with the Soviet.

The U.S.A. is still hoarding larger and larger quantities of Gold. It does not seem to occur to her economists that to exchange goods for Gold, which is buried in their Bank Vaults and is "sterilized" to use the Stock Exchange jargon, is to give away their goods for nothing. Trade is the exchange of goods which have a utility value for other goods which have a utility value, and sterilized gold has no utility value at all.

As long as Gold is still regarded as wealth by the mass of mankind, it is thought necessary for a trading nation to have a Gold reserve, but Germany - deprived by her creditors of all her Gold - has challenged that idea and is building up an export trade without it and is to-day our largest customer.

Germany has not only challenged the political system of the Democracies but the economic system of international finance and international monopolies, and it is to that challenge that all the attacks in the Press and the attempts to force the people of this country into war are due.

If Germany succeeds in her economic system of basing her currency on labour values and exchanging goods for goods, the whole of the Gold stored in the Bank vaults of the U.S.A. can be written off as a dead loss, and Gold mining which depends on selling Gold at a higher and higher price to the Governments who buy the Gold bars and do nothing with them, will collapse. The old story of King Midas who starved because everything he touched turned to Gold will come true.

The German Government has shown that Gold is not necessary and that is one of the reasons for the policy pursued against them by Great Britain, France and the U.S.A. Millions are being spent on this propaganda, but when once the peoples of Great Britain, France and the U.S.A. realise that the cry that Germany aims at universal dominion is a lie to-day just as it was a lie in 1914; that the only danger facing Democracy is its own misrule, weakness in the face of vested interests and sacrifice of public interest to the greedy scramble of politicians for power; that they are being driven like sheep to the slaughter by big finance just as they were driven into the Boer war, they will turn in revolt. The revolt has already begun in England though not reported by our Press.

Germany has symbolized international finance by calling it "the Jew". It is true Jews are to a great extent interested. International finance is the public enemy and the promoter of war among the peoples, but those controlling it belong to all nations, and it is centred in London, Paris and New York. The "City" rules this country. They threw the Labour Party out of power when it suited them, and they control our Government today. When Roosevelt and our Government say they are willing to consider how to set free the supply of raw materials they are

THE CASE FOR GERMANY.

promising what they cannot perform as they are helpless in the grip of the huge combines. Only the Totalitarian States are free states. King Midas is the Public Enemy number one.

While the Monopolists combine to accumulate Gold it is no longer the basis of their paper currency. We have ourselves abolished the ratio between Gold and paper, and France devalues the Franc at intervals. The confusion between the world currencies continues and will end in a collapse. The only sound currency to-day is the German currency.

It is also necessary for the world to return in some form or other to Free Trade, but it must be a Free Trade that does not cause a competition between different standards of living. Germany has solved these problems by exchanging goods for goods based on barter.

Before these international questions are discussed the Monopolists have to ask themselves why, with the world wealth in their possession, they suffer from serious unemployment, which has reached in the U.S.A. the appalling figure of 20 million people on the dole, while Germany has to hire surplus labour abroad. They must reform their own economic system before they reform the world.

They have also to ask themselves two very fundamental questions, namely, is it possible to combine the Democratic idea with the principle that the first duty of the citizen is the welfare of the community, and with honest government not controlled behind the scenes by the Financiers.

Democracies are in many cases financially corrupt Governments. In our case that is not true but our Government and Parliament are intellectually dishonest. Truth is sacrificed every day to a party advantage. If lies were only consciously told it would not be so serious but political life produces a mental degeneration in which it is no longer possible for the politicians to distinguish between truth and falsehood.

An excellent example occurred in the House of Commons the other day when the leaders of the Opposition accused Franco of dropping from his planes chocolate boxes containing infernal machines so that when children picked them up they were blown to pieces. Men who can say such things are really mentally insane and these champions of Democracy are our rulers to whom we submit the safety of our State.

The Parliamentary system is becoming unworkable. The Peoples of the Democracies, owing to the iron control of publicity, are dumb and can be driven to war without a protest. Even a pig is allowed to squeal before he is killed.

We shall owe to Germany not only the abolition of the Politician, but a new ethical conception of a community, Peace in Europe and a reformed economic and trading system which will reconstruct world economics and abolish the evil influences of international finance and huge trading monopolies.

The great speech made by the Führer has deflated the war balloon blown out with poison gas by the Press. Germany makes no threat of war against any nation. The war anxiety among the small nations of Europe is not due to German action but to the uncertainty as to whether we do not intend to provoke war and the fear of our hysterical and unbalanced Democracy, for they know that Great Britain is dangerous when she is filled with moral indignation at the sins of her neighbours. When the giants are fighting the small nations will suffer.

It is true Holland is busy arming her frontier facing Germany but she is just as busy arming her harbours facing England. France is evidently hesitating between Peace, Trade and friendship with Germany and being further involved in our reckless foreign policy. It is said that our beginning of conscription is the price we are paying to keep her with us. Before finally considering the two policies put before the peoples of Europe and the peoples of this country by the Führer and the British Government respectively, let us briefly look at the present condition of Europe as revealed by our attempts to consolidate it in a new policy against Germany.

Switzerland, Belgium, Holland, Denmark, Norway, Sweden, Finland, Estonia, Latvia and Lithuania deny that they fear any act [of] aggression on the part of Germany, refuse to be drawn into any alliance that may commit them to war, and state that if war comes they will remain neutral.

Germany, Italy, Spain, Slovakia, Hungary and Jugoslavia are united in the closest bonds of friendship and mutual confidence. Rumania and Greece, while not refusing our offer of assistance if attacked, will not sign a Treaty which will in any way commit them to war.

A chain of Peace Pacts beginning in Italy joins Italy to Jugoslavia, Jugoslavia to Bulgaria, Bulgaria to Turkey.

Poland alone has formed a mutual security pact with us, and by so doing broken her Peace Pact with Germany.

France is isolated in Europe to-day and has chosen to quarrel with her three neighbours on her frontiers - Spain, Italy and Germany. This attitude of hostility can be ended when she chooses, and grants the quite reasonable requests of Italy.

Before Hitler rose to power all countries in Europe had armed and a criss cross of mutual security pacts made war possible and no one could say where it would stop. Since Germany rose to power the consolidation of Europe into friendly nations promoting trade has proceeded apace. A central area of Europe from the frontiers of Holland to the frontiers of Rumania, and united to Italy and Spain is settled as a permanent area of Peace, - an area equal to the old Austrian Empire and united to Germany by friendship, not by dominance of a central Government. If Germany and Italy acting jointly are able to settle the differences about land frontiers between Hungary and Rumania, this will extend to the Black Sea.

Formerly Poland could be included. Unfortunately for her she has broken away owing to our interference. This Pax Germanica which is gradually extending over Europe is the work of two men - Hitler and Mussolini.

Let us now consider the two policies offered by Hitler on the one hand and our Government on the other.

To Hitler we owe the idea of Peace Pacts. Two nations agree not to go to war for a term of years. This does not involve any alliance against a third Power. This policy has spread over Europe and into Asia. Turkey, Iraq, Persia and Afghanistan are united by Peace Pacts.

The first Peace Pact between Germany and Poland resulted in the friendly settlement of very delicate and difficult points and it is disastrous for her that Poland has broken it.

The other policy of mutual security pacts is simply the Policy of Treaties between two nations directed *against* a third nation under a new name which existed before the war and had such disastrous consequences. Germany was bound to Austria, England was bound to France, and France to Russia, and so an insignificant Balkan war involved all Europe in a catastrophe. This policy was tried during the reign of the League and produced unrest and fear of war all over Europe. It means the assumption by a nation of obligations to fight for a foreign policy over which it has no control, and it ensures automatically a local war between two powers involving all those linked by mutual security pacts. A break at any point in the complicated chain involves the whole in disaster. It means dividing Europe into two hostile camps, which must end in war sooner or later.

Hitler has always denounced mutual security and Germany beyond her guarantee of the integrity of Belgium and of Slovakia is free from all such commitments. Our alliance with France has been disastrous to both countries as neither country is free to follow the foreign policy suited to its own interests. It is, for instance, essential for France today to develop friendly relations with Spain and Italy, and above all with Germany. Many intelligent Frenchmen curse the alliance with us dragging France into our disastrous and reckless Foreign Policy.

The peoples of Europe, of Great Britain and the British Empire have the chance of adopting the policy of Hitler and Peace, or of Chamberlain who is being driven by forces hostile to Germany to war. I thank God that the Peace of Europe is in the guardianship of the Führer and therefore, in spite of the frantic efforts of all those here and in Europe and America who want war, secure.

Epilogue by The Scriptorium, November 11, 2003

These closing words were written in June 1939. As we all know, things turned out rather differently than Dr. Laurie expected, and at the time of his writing the remaining days of peace were already numbered at less than 100. It seems appropriate, therefore, to close this book with just a few words from the most virulent of those men who wanted the developments the world actually got, and who with their frantic efforts succeeded in thwarting what could have been a long and prosperous European and global peace:

Lord Vansittart, at the time of this quote Permanent Under-Secretary at the British Foreign Office: "If Hitler fails, his successor will be Bolshevism; if he is successful, we will present him with a European war within five years." In his book *Even now,* London **1933**, p. 69. [Note how close the predicted timing was to actual fact!]

Lord Dawson of Penn, in conversation with Swedish explorer Sven Hedin on July 25, **1939** in Stockholm:
Dawson: "The moment that Germany occupies Danzig - whether it be by peaceful means, or with armed force - we will immediately and absolutely declare war on Germany."
Sven Hedin: "A world war, for Danzig? Danzig is a German city, and the injustices of the Treaty of Versailles are being revised."
Dawson: "[...] if Danzig falls, it's a matter of the life of the British Empire. We know that **a new world war for the sake of Danzig is more than due, and we will take the opportunity when it presents itself.**"
Sven Hedin: "Are you prepared to take such a responsibility?"
Dawson: "**We understand that there will be nothing left of civilization afterwards, but we will not hesitate one instant.**"
(As quoted in Friedrich Lenz, *Worm in the Apple,* 1997, ch. 7.)

Winston Churchill, British Prime Minister: "Germany is becoming too strong. We must crush her." Said to American General Robert E. Wood in November **1936.** And: "This war is a British war and its goal is the destruction of Germany." Said in **November 1939** in a radio address to the British people. And **just a short time later:** "You must understand that this war is not against Hitler or National Socialism, but against the strength of the German people, which is to be smashed for good regardless of whether it is in the hands of Hitler or a Jesuit priest." Latter quoted in E. Hughes, *Winston Churchill - His Career in War and Peace,* p. 145.

Duff Cooper, First Lord of the Admiralty and British Minister for Information: "The coming peace treaty must be much harsher and more merciless than Versailles. We can make no distinction between Hitler and the German people!" Said on April 25, **1940,** as quoted in: Father E. J. Reichenberger, *Wider Willkür und Machtrausch,* 1955, p. 114.

The list could go on...

23

Appendix

On National Socialism And World Relations.
Speech delivered in the German Reichstag on January 30th 1937
by Adolf Hitler, Führer and Chancellor

[**Scriptorium notes:** This Appendix was missing from our copy of Dr. Laurie's book and has been added here by The Scriptorium as a translation based on the German-language original as recorded in the Proceedings of the Reichstag. See wintersonnenwende.com for select *Verhandlungen des Reichstags* in the German original.]

This session of the Reichstag takes place on a date which is full of significance for the German people. Four years have passed since the beginning of that great internal revolution which in the meantime has been giving a new aspect to German life. This is the period of four years which I asked the German people to grant me for the purpose of putting my work to the test and submitting it to their judgement. Hence at the present moment nothing could be more opportune than for me to render you an account of all the successes that have been achieved and the progress that has been made during these four years, for the welfare of the German people. But within the limits of the short statement I have to make it would be entirely impossible to enumerate all the remarkable results that have been reached during a time which may be looked upon as probably the most astounding epoch in the life of our people. That task belongs rather to the press and the propaganda. Moreover, during the course of the present year there will be an Exposition here in Berlin which is being organized for the purpose of giving a more comprehensive and detailed picture of the works that have been completed, the results that have been obtained and the projects on which work has been begun, all of which can be explained better in this way than I could do it within the limits of an address that is to last for two hours. Therefore I shall utilize the opportunity afforded me by this historic meeting of the Reichstag to cast a glance back over the past four years and call attention to some of the new knowledge that we have gained, some of the experiences which we have been through, and the consequences that have resulted therefrom - in so far as these have a general validity. It is important that we should understand them clearly, not only for our own sake but also for that of the generations to come.

Having done this, I shall pass on to explain our attitude towards those problems and tasks whose importance for us and for the world around us must be appreciated before it will be possible to live in better relations with one another. Finally I should like to describe as briefly as possible the projects which I have before my mind for our work in the near future and indeed in the distant future also.

At the time when I used to go here and there throughout the country, simply as a public speaker, people from the bourgeois classes used to ask me why we believed that a revolution would be necessary, instead of working within the framework of the established political order and with the collaboration of the parties already in existence, for the purpose of improving those conditions which we considered unsound and injurious. Why must we have a new party, and especially why a new revolution? The answer which I then gave may be stated under the following headings:

1. The elements of confusion and dissolution which are making themselves felt in German life, in the concept of life itself and the will to national self-preservation, cannot be eradicated by a mere change of government. More than enough of those changes have already taken place without bringing about any essential betterment of the distress that exists in Germany. All these Cabinet reconstructions brought some positive advantage only to the actors who took part in the play; but the results were almost always quite negative as far as the interests of the people were concerned. As time has gone on the thought and practical life of our people have been led astray into ways that are unnatural to them, and injurious. One of the causes which brought about this condition of affairs must be attributed to the fact that the structure of our State and our methods of government were foreign to our own national character, our historical development and our national needs.

The parliamentary-democratic system is inseparable from the other symptoms of the time. A critical situation cannot be remedied by collaborating with the causes of it but by a radical extermination of these causes. Hence under such conditions the political struggle must necessarily take the form of a revolution.

2. It is out of the question to think that such a revolutionary reconstruction could be carried out by those who are the custodians and the more or less responsible representatives of the old regime, or by the political organizations founded under the old form of the Constitution. Nor would it be possible to bring this about by collaborating with these institutions, but only by establishing a new movement which will fight against them for the purpose of carrying through a radical reformation in political, cultural and economic life. And this fight will have to be undertaken even at the sacrifice of life and blood, if that should be necessary.

In this connection it is worthy of remark that when the average political party wins a parliamentary victory no essential change takes place in the historical course which the people are following, or in the outer aspect of public life; whereas a genuine revolution that arises from a profound ideological insight will always lead to a transformation which is strikingly impressive and is manifest to the outside world. Surely nobody will doubt the fact that during the last four years a revolution of the most momentous character has passed like a storm over Germany. Who could compare this new Germany with that which existed on the 30th. of January four years ago, when I took my oath of loyalty before the venerable President of the Reich?

I am speaking of a National Socialist Revolution; but this revolutionary process in Germany had a particular character of its own, which may have been the reason why the outside world and so many of our fellow-countrymen failed to understand the profound nature of the transformation that took place. I do not deny that this peculiar feature, which has been for us the most outstanding characteristic of the lines along which the National Socialist Revolution took place - a feature which we can be specially proud of - has hindered rather than helped to make this unique historic event understood abroad and among some of our own people. For the National Socialist Revolution was in itself a revolution in the revolutionary tradition.

What I mean is this: Throughout thousands of years the conviction grew up and prevailed, not so much in the German mind as in the minds of the contemporary world, that bloodshed and the extermination of those hitherto in power - together with the destruction of public and private institutions and property - were essential characteristics of every true revolution. Mankind in general has grown accustomed to accept revolutions with all these consequences somehow or other as if they were legal happenings. I do not mean that people endorse all this tumultuous destruction of life and property; but they certainly accept it as the necessary accompaniment of events which, because of this very reason, are called revolutions.

Herein lies the difference between the National Socialist Revolution and other revolutions, with the exception of the Fascist Revolution in Italy. The National Socialist Revolution was almost entirely a bloodless proceeding. When the party took over power in Germany, after overthrowing the very formidable obstacles that had stood in its way, it did so without causing any damage whatsoever to property. I can say with a certain amount of pride that this was the first revolution in which not even a window-pane was broken.

Don't misunderstand me, however. If this revolution was bloodless that was not because we were not manly enough to look at blood.

I was a soldier for more than four years in a war where more blood was shed than ever before throughout human history. I never lost my nerve, no matter what the situation was and no matter what sights I had to face. The same holds good for my party colleagues. But we did not consider it as part of the programme of the National Socialist Revolution to destroy human life or material goods, but rather to build up a new and better life. And it is the greatest source of pride to us that we have been able to carry through this revolution, which is certainly the greatest revolution ever experienced in the history of our people, with a minimum of loss and sacrifice. Only in those cases where the murderous lust of the Bolsheviks, even after the 30th of January 1933, led them to think that by the use of brute force they could prevent the success and realization of the National Socialist ideal - only then did we answer violence with violence, and naturally we did it promptly. Certain other individuals of a naturally undisciplined temperament, and who had no political consciousness whatsoever, had to be taken into protective custody; but, generally speaking, these individuals were given their freedom after a short period. Beyond this there was a small number who took part in politics only for the purpose of establishing an alibi for their criminal activities, which were proved by the numerous sentences to prison and penal servitude that had been passed upon them previously. We prevented such individuals from pursuing their destructive careers, inasmuch as we set them to do some useful work, probably for the first time in their lives.

I do not know if there ever has been a resolution which was of such a profound character as the National Socialist Revolution and which at the same time allowed innumerable persons who had been prominent in political circles under the former regime to follow their respective callings in private life peacefully and without causing them any worry. Not only that, but even many among our bitterest enemies, some of whom had occupied the highest positions in the government, were allowed to enjoy their regular emoluments and pensions.

That is what we did. But this policy did not always help our reputation abroad. Just a few months ago we had an experience with some very honourable British world-citizens who considered themselves obliged to address a protest to me because I had some criminal protégés of the Moscow regime interned in a German concentration camp. Perhaps it is because I am not very well informed on current affairs that I have not heard whether those honourable gentlemen have ever expressed their indignation at the various acts of sanguinary violence which these Moscow criminals committed in Germany, or whether they ever expressed themselves against the slogan: "Strike down and kill the Fascist wherever you meet him", or whether, for example, they have taken the occasion of recent happenings in Spain to express their indignation against slaughtering and violating and burning to death thousands upon thousands of men, women and children. If the revolution in Germany had taken place according to the democratic model in Spain these strange apostles of non-intervention abroad would probably find that there was nothing which they need to worry about. People closely acquainted with the state of affairs in Spain have assured us that if we place the number of persons who have been slaughtered in this bestial way at 170,000, the figure will probably be too low rather than too high. Measured by the achievements of the noble democratic revolutionaries in Spain, the quota of human beings allotted for slaughter to the National Socialist Revolution would have been about 400,000 or 500,000; because our population is about three times larger than that of Spain. That we did not carry out this mass-slaughter is apparently looked on as a piece of negligence on our part. We see that the democratic world-citizens are by no means gracious in their criticism of this leniency.

We certainly had the power in our hands to do what has been done in Spain. And probably we had better nerves than the murderer who steals upon his victim unawares, shunning the open fight, and who is capable only of murdering defenceless hostages. We have been soldiers and we never flinched in the face of battle throughout that most gruesome war of all times. Our hearts and, I may also add, our sound common sense saved us from committing any acts like those which have been done in Spain.

Taking it all in all, fewer lives were sacrificed in the National Socialist Revolution than the number of National Socialist followers who were murdered in Germany by our Bolshevik opponents in the year 1932 alone, when there was no revolution.

This absence of bloodshed and destruction was made possible solely because we had adopted a principle which not only guided our conduct in the past but which we shall also never forget in the future. This principle was that the purpose of a revolution, or of any general change in the condition of public affairs, cannot be to produce chaos but only to replace what is bad by substituting something better. In such cases, however, something better must be ready at hand. On the 30th of January four years ago, when the venerable President of the Reich sent for me and entrusted me with the task of forming a new Cabinet, we had already come through a strenuous struggle in our efforts to obtain supreme political control over the State. All the means employed in carrying on that struggle were strictly within the law as it then stood and the protagonists in the fight were the National Socialists. Before the new State could be actually established and promulgated, the idea of it and the model for its organisation had already existed within the framework of our party. All the fundamental principles on which the new Reich was to be constructed were the principles and ideas already embodied in the National Socialist Party.

As a result of the constitutional struggle to win over our German fellow-countrymen to our side the party had established its predominance in the Reichstag and for a whole year before it actually assumed power it already had the right to demand this power for itself, even according to the principles of the parliamentary-democratic system.

But it was essential for the National Socialist Revolution that this party should put forward demands which of themselves would involve a real revolutionary change in the principles and institutions of government hitherto in force.

When certain individuals who were blind to the actual state of affairs thought that they could refuse to submit to the practical application of the principles of the movement which had been entrusted with the government of the Reich, then, but not until then, the party used an iron hand to make these illegal disturbers of the peace bend their stubborn necks before the laws of the new National Socialist Reich and Government.

With this act the National Socialist Revolution came to an end. For as soon as the party had taken over power, and this new condition of affairs was consolidated, I looked upon it as a matter of course that the Revolution should be transformed into an evolution.

The new development which now set in, however, meant that there had to be a new orientation not merely of our ideas but also in regard to the practical policy which we had to carry out. Even today certain individuals who have fallen in the march of events refuse to adapt themselves to this change. They cannot understand it because it is beyond their mental horizon or outside the sphere of their egotistic interests. Our National Socialist teaching has undoubtedly a revolutionizing effect in many spheres of life and has interfered and acted under the revolutionary impulse.

The main plank in the National Socialist programme is to abolish the liberalistic concept of the individual and the Marxist concept of humanity and to substitute therefore the folk community, rooted in the soil and bound together by the bond of its common blood. A very simple statement; but it involves a principle that has tremendous consequences.

This is probably the first time and this is the first country in which people are being taught to realize that, of all the tasks which we have to face, the noblest and most sacred for mankind is that each racial species must preserve the purity of the blood which God has given it.

And thus it happens that for the first time it is now possible for men to use their God-given faculties of perception and insight in the understanding of those problems which are of more momentous importance for the preservation of human existence than all the victories that may be won on the battlefield or the successes that may be obtained through economic efforts. The greatest revolution which National Socialism has brought about is that it has rent asunder the veil which hid from us the knowledge that all human failures and mistakes are due to the conditions of the time and therefore can be remedied, but that there is one error which cannot be remedied once men have made it, namely the failure to recognize the importance of conserving the blood and the race free from intermixture and thereby the racial aspect and character which are God's gift and God's handiwork. It is not for men to discuss the question of why Providence created different races, but rather to recognise the fact that it punishes those who disregard its work of creation.

Unspeakable suffering and misery have come upon mankind because they lost this instinct which was grounded in a profound intuition; and this loss was caused by a wrong and lopsided education of the intellect. Among our people there are millions and millions of persons living today for whom this law has become clear and intelligible. What individual seers and the still unspoiled natures of our forefathers saw by direct perception has now become a subject of scientific research in Germany. And I can prophesy here that, just as the knowledge that the earth moves around the sun led to a revolutionary alternation in the general world-picture, so the blood-and-race doctrine of the National Socialist Movement will bring about a revolutionary change in our knowledge and therewith a radical reconstruction of the picture which human history gives us of the past and will also change the course of that history in the future.

And this will not lead to an estrangement between the nations; but, on the contrary, it will bring about for the first time a real understanding of one another. At the same time, however, it will prevent the Jewish people from intruding themselves among all the other nations as elements of internal disruption, under the mask of honest world-citizens, and thus gaining power over these nations.

We feel convinced that the consequences of this really revolutionising vision of truth will bring about a radical transformation in German life. For the first time in our history, the German people have found the way to a higher unity than they ever had before; and that is due to the compelling attraction of this inner feeling. Innumerable prejudices have been broken down, many barriers have been overthrown as unreasonable, evil traditions have been wiped out and antiquated symbols shown to be meaningless. From that chaos of disunion which had been caused by tribal, dynastic, philosophical, religious and political strife, the German nation has arisen and has unfurled the banner of a reunion which symbolically announces, not a political triumph, but the triumph of the racial principle. For the past four-and-a-half years German legislation has upheld and enforced this idea. Just as on January 30th, 1933, a state of affairs already in existence was legalized by the fact that I was entrusted with the chancellorship, whereby the party whose supremacy in Germany had then become unquestionable was now authorized to take over the government of the Reich and mould the future destiny of Germany; so this German legislation that has been in force for the past four years was only the legal sanction which gave jurisdiction and binding force to an idea that had already been clearly formulated and promulgated by the party.

When the German community, based on the racial blood-bond, became realised in the German State we all felt that this would remain one of the finest moments to be remembered during our lives. Like a blast of springtime it passed over Germany four years ago. The fighting forces of our movement who for many years had defended the banner of the Hooked Cross against the superior forces of the enemy, and had carried it steadily forward for a long fourteen years, now planted it firmly in the soil of the new Reich.

Within a few weeks the political debris and the social prejudices which had been accumulating through a thousand years of German history were removed and cleared away.

May we not speak of a revolution when the chaotic conditions brought about by parliamentary democracy disappear in less than three months and a regime of order and discipline takes their place, and a new energy springs forth from a firmly welded unity and a comprehensive authoritative power such as Germany never before had?

So great was the Revolution that its intellectual foundations are not even yet understood but are superficially criticized by our contemporaries. They talk of democracies and dictatorships; but they fail to grasp the fact that in this country a radical transformation has taken place and has produced results which are democratic in the highest sense of the word, if democracy has any meaning at all.

With infallible certainty we are steering towards an order of things in which a process of selection will become active in the political leadership of the nation, as it exists throughout the whole of life in general. By this process of selection, which will follow the laws of Nature and the dictates of human reason, those among our people who show the greatest natural ability will be appointed to positions in the political leadership of the nation. In making this selection no consideration will be given to birth or ancestry, name or wealth, but only to the question of whether or not the candidate has a natural vocation for those higher positions of leadership. It was a fine principle which the great Corsican enunciated when he said that each one of his soldiers carried a marshal's baton in the haversack. In this country that principle will have its political counterpart. Is there a nobler or more excellent kind of Socialism and is there a truer form of Democracy than this National Socialism which is so organised that through it each one among the millions of German boys is given the possibility of finding his way to the highest office in the nation, should it please Providence to come to his aid?

And that is no theory. In the present National Socialist Germany it is a reality that is considered by us all as a matter of course. I myself, to whom the people have given their trust and who have been called to be their leader, come from the people. All the millions of German workers know that it is not a foreign dilettante or an international revolutionary apostle who is at the head of the Reich, but a German who has come from their own ranks.

And numerous people whose families belong to the peasantry and working classes are now filling prominent positions in this National Socialist State. Some of them actually hold the highest offices in the leadership of the nation, as Cabinet Ministers, *Reichsstatthalter* and *Gauleiter*. But National Socialism always bears in mind the interests of the people as a whole and not the interests of one class or another.

The National Socialist Revolution has not aimed at turning a privileged class into a class which will have no rights in the future. Its aim has been to grant equal rights to those social strata that hitherto were denied such rights. We have not ruined millions of citizens by degrading them to the level of enslaved workers. Our aim has been to educate slaves to be German citizens. One thing will certainly be quite clear to every German; and this is that revolutions as acts of terror can only be of short duration. If revolutions are not able to produce something new they will end up by devouring the whole of the national patrimony which existed before them. From the assumption of power as an act of force the beneficial work of peace must be promptly developed. But those who abolish classes for the purpose of putting new classes in their place sow the seeds of new revolutions. The bourgeois citizen who has the ruling power in his hands today will become a proletarian if he is banished to Siberia tomorrow and condemned to enforced labour there. He will then yearn for his day of deliverance, just as did the proletarian of former times, who now thinks that his turn has come to play the despot. Therefore the National Socialist Revolution never aimed at bringing in one class of the German people and turning out another. One the contrary, our objective has been to make it possible

THE CASE FOR GERMANY.

for the whole German people to work, not only in the economic but also in the political field, and to guarantee this possibility by organising the various classes into one national unit.

The National Socialist Movement, however, limits its sphere of internal activity to those individuals who belong to one people and it refuses to allow the members of a foreign race to wield an influence over our political, intellectual, or cultural life. And we refuse to accord to the members of a foreign race any predominant position in our national economic system.

In this folk-community, which is based on the bond of blood, and in the results which National Socialism has obtained by making the idea of this community understood among the public, lies the most profound reason for the marvelous success of our Revolution.

Confronted with this new and vigorous ideal, all idols and relics of the past which had been upheld by dynastic interests, tribal affiliations and even party interests, now began to lose their glamour. That is why the whole party system of former times completely collapsed in a few weeks, without giving rise to the feeling that something had been lost. They were superseded by a better ideal. A new movement took their place. A re-organisation of our people into a national unit that includes all those whose labour is productive simply pushed aside the old organisations of employers and employees. The symbolic emblems of the recent past, which was a period of disintegration and disability, were banished, not - as in 1918 or 1919 - through a resolution voted by a committee appointed to invent a new symbol for the Reich, as if the choice were to depend on the results of a prize competition. But all these old emblems were now displaced by that flag which symbolised the militant period of the National Socialist Movement and which was borne by us on the day of Germany's resurgence. Since that day it has become the consecrated symbol of this national resurgence on land and sea and in the air.

There could be no more eloquent proof of how profoundly the German people have understood the significance of this change and new development than the manner in which the nation sanctioned our regime at the polls on so many occasions during the years that followed. So, of all those who like to point again and again to the democratic form of government as the institution which is based on the universal will of the people, in contrast to dictatorships, nobody has a better right to speak in the name of the people than I have.

Among the results of this phase of the German Revolution I may enumerate the following:

1. Since that time there is only one bearer of state sovereignty, namely the entire German people themselves.

2. The will of this people finds its expression in the Party as the political organisation of this people.

3. Accordingly, there is only one single legislative power.

4. There is only one executive power.

Whoever compares this with Germany prior to January 1933 will see what a great transformation is embodied in these few short statements.

But this transformation is only a result that has followed from carrying a fundamental axiom of the National Socialist doctrine into practical effect. This axiom is that the only reasonable meaning and purpose of all human thought and conduct cannot be to create or to maintain structures, organisations or functions made by men, but only to preserve and develop the innate character of the people itself; for Providence has given us this character as the groundwork of all our constructive efforts. Through the successful issue of the National Socialist Movement the people as such was placed above any organisation, construction or function, as the sole element that is always there and will permanently abide. The meaning and purpose which Providence had in mind when it created the different races cannot be investigated by us, human beings, and no theory about it can be laid down. But the meaning and purpose of human organisations and of all human activities can be measured by asking what value they are for the maintenance of the race or people, which is the one existing element that must abide. The people - the race - is the primary thing. Party, State, Army, the national economic structure, Justice etc, all these are only secondary and accidental. They are only the means to the end and the end is the preservation of this nation. These public institutions are right and useful according to the measure in which their energies are directed towards this task. If they are incapable of fulfilling it, then their existence is harmful and they must either be reformed or removed and replaced by something better.

It is absolutely necessary that this principle should be practically recognised; for that is the only way in which men can be saved from becoming the victims of a devitalized set of dogmas in a matter where dogmas are entirely out of place, and from drawing dogmatic conclusions from the consideration of ways and means, when the final purpose itself is the only valid dogma.

All of you, gentlemen and members of the German Reichstag, understand the meaning of what I have just said. But on this occasion I am speaking to the whole German people and therefore I should like to bring forward a few examples which show how important these principles were proved to be when they were put into practice. There are many people for whom this is the only way of explaining why we talk of a Nationalist Socialist Revolution, though no blood was shed and no property wrecked.

For a long time our ideas of law and justice had been developing in a way that led to a state of general confusion. This was partly due to the fact that we adopted ideas which were foreign to our national character and also partly because the German mind itself did not have any clear notion of what public justice meant. This confusion was evidenced more strikingly by the lack of inner clarity as to the function of law and justice.

There are two extreme poles which are characteristic of this mental lack:

1. The opinion that the law as such is its own justification and hence cannot be made the subject of any critical analysis as to its utility, either in regard to its general principles or its relation to particular problems. According to this notion, the law would remain even though the world should disappear.

2. The opinion that it is the main function of law to protect and safeguard the life and property of the individual.

Between these two extreme poles the idea of defending the larger interests of the community was introduced very timidly and under the cloak of an appeal to reasons of state.

In contradistinction to all this, the National Socialist Revolution has laid down a definite and unambiguous principle on which the whole system of legislation, jurisprudence and administration of justice must be founded.

It is the task of justice to collaborate in supporting and protecting the people as a whole against those individuals who, because they lack a social conscience, try to shirk the obligations to which all the members of the community are subject, or directly act against the interests of the community itself.

In the new German legal system which will be in force from now onwards the nation is placed above persons and property.

The principle expressed in that brief statement and everything it implies has led to the greatest reform ever introduced in our German legal structure. The first decisive action taken in accordance with the fundamental principle I have spoken of was the setting up not only of one legislator but also of one executive. The second measure is not yet ready but will be announced to the nation within a few weeks.

In the German penal code, which has been drawn up with this wide general perspective in view, German justice will be placed for the first time on a basis which ensures that for all time to come its duty will be to serve in maintaining the German race.

THE CASE FOR GERMANY.

Although the chaos which we found before us in the various branches of public life was very great indeed, the state of dissolution into which German economic life had fallen was still greater. And this was the feature of the German collapse that impressed itself most strikingly on the minds of the broad masses of the people. The conditions that then actually existed have still remained in their memories and in the memory of the German people as a whole. As outstanding examples of this catastrophe we found these two phenomena:

1. More than six millions of unemployed.
2. An agricultural population that was manifestly doomed to dissolution.

The area covered by the German agricultural farms that were on the point of being sold up by forced auction was as large as the whole of Thuringia (more than 8,000 square miles).

In the natural course of events the falling off in production on the one side, and the decrease in purchasing power on the other, must necessarily bring about the disruption and annihilation of the great mass of the middle class also. How seriously this side of the German distress was then felt might subsequently be measured by the fact that I had to ask for the period of four years especially for the purpose of reducing unemployment and putting a stop to the dissolution of the German agricultural population.

I may further state that in 1933 the National Socialists did not interfere with any activities which were being carried out by others and which at the same time promised success. The Party was called to take over the government of the country at a moment when the possibilities of redeeming the situation in any other way had been exhausted and particularly when repeated attempts to overcome the economic crisis had failed.

After four years from that date I now face the German people and you, gentlemen and members of the Reichstag, to give an account of what has been accomplished. On this occasion I do not think you will withhold your sanction from what the National Socialist Government has done and you will agree that I have fulfilled the promises I made four years ago.

It was not an easy undertaking. I am not giving away any secrets when I tell you that at that time the so-called economic experts were convinced that the economic crisis could not be overcome. In the face of this staggering situation which, as I have said, appeared hopeless to the minds of the experts, I still believed in the possibility of a German revival and particularly in the possibility of an economic recovery. My belief was grounded on two considerations:

1. I have always had only pity for those excited people who invariably talk of the collapse of the nation whenever they find themselves confronted with a difficult situation. What do they mean by a collapse? The German people were already in existence before they made any definite appearance in history as it is known to us. Now, leaving out entirely what their pre-historic experiences may have been, it is certain that during the past two thousand years of history, through which that portion of mankind which we call the German People has passed, unspeakable miseries and catastrophes must have befallen them more than once. Famines, wars and pestilences have overwhelmed our people and wreaked terrible havoc among them. It must give rise to unlimited faith in the vital resources of a nation when we recall the fact that only a few centuries ago our German people, with a population of more than eighteen millions, were reduced by the Thirty Years War to less than four millions. Let us also remember that this once flourishing land was pillaged, dismembered and devastated, that its cities were burned down, its hamlets and villages laid waste, that its fields were left uncultivated and barren. Some ten years afterwards our people began again to increase in number. The cities were rebuilt and began to be filled with a new life. The fields were ploughed once more. Songs were heard along the countryside, in concord with the rhythm of that work which brought new life and livelihood to the people.

Let us look back over the development, or at least that part of it known to us, through which our people have passed since those dim historic ages down to the present time. We shall then recognise how puny is all the fuss that these weakling footlers make who immediately begin to talk about the collapse of the economic structure - and hence of human existence - the first moment a piece of printed paper loses its face value somewhere in the world. Germany and the German people have mastered many a grave catastrophe. Of course, we must admit that the right men were always needed to formulate the necessary measures and enforce them without paying any attention to those negative persons who always think that they know more than others. A bevy of parliamentarian weaklings are certainly not the kind of men to lead a nation out of the slough of distress and despair. I firmly believed and was solemnly convinced that the economic catastrophe would be mastered in Germany as soon as the people could be got to believe in their own immortality as a people and as soon as they realised that the aim and purpose of all economic effort is to save and maintain the life of the nation.

2. I was not an economist, which means that I have never been a theorist during my whole life.

But unfortunately I have observed that the worst theorists are always busy in those quarters where theory has no place at all and where practical life counts for everything. It goes without saying that in the economic sphere and with the passing of time experience has given rise to the employment of certain definite principles and also definite methods of work which have been proved to be productive of good results. But all methods and principles are subject to the time element. To make hard-and-fast dogmas out of practical methods would deprive the human faculties and working power of that elasticity which alone enables them to face changing demands by changing the means of meeting them accordingly and thus mastering them. There were many persons among us who busied themselves, with that perseverance which is characteristic of the Germans, in an effort to formulate dogmas from economic methods and then raise that dogmatic system to a branch of our university curriculum, under the title of national economy. According to the pronouncements issued by these national economists, Germany was irrevocably lost. It is a characteristic of all dogmatists that they vigorously reject any new dogma. In other words, they criticise any new piece of knowledge that may be put forward and reject it as mere theory. For the last eighteen years we have been witnessing a rare spectacle. Our economic dogmatists have been proved wrong in almost every branch of practical life and yet they repudiate those who have actually overcome the economic crisis, as propagators of false theories and damn them accordingly.

You all know the story of the doctor who told a patient that he could live only for another six months. Ten years afterwards the patient met the physician; but the only surprise which the latter expressed at the recovery of the patient was to state that the treatment which the second doctor gave the patient was entirely wrong.

The German economic policy which National Socialism introduced in 1933 is based on some fundamental considerations. In the relations between economics and the people, the people alone is the only unchangeable element. Economic activity in itself is no dogma and never can be such.

There is no economic theory or opinion which can claim to be considered as sacrosanct. The will to place the economic system at the service of the people, and capital at the service of economics, is the only thing that is of decisive importance here.

We know that National Socialism vigorously combats the opinion which holds that the economic structure exists for the benefit of capital and that the people are to be looked upon as subject to the economic system. We were therefore determined from the very beginning to exterminate the false notion that the economic system could exist and operate entirely freely and entirely outside of any control or supervision on the part of the State. Today there can no longer be such a thing as an independent economic system. That is to say, the economic system can no longer be left to itself exclusively. And this is so, not only because it is unallowable from the political point of view but also because, in the purely economic sphere itself, the consequences would be disastrous.

It is out of the question that millions of individuals should be allowed to work just as they like and merely to meet their own needs; but it is just as impossible to allow the entire system of economics to function according to the notions held exclusively in economic circles and thus made to serve egotistic interests. Then there is the further consideration that these economic circles are not in a position to bear the responsibility for their own failures. In its modern phase of the development, the economic system concentrates enormous masses of workers in certain special branches and in definite local areas. New inventions or a slump in the market may destroy whole branches of industry at one blow.

The industrialist may close his factory gates. He may even try to find a new field for his personal activities. In most cases he will not be ruined so easily. Moreover, the industrialists who have to suffer in such contingencies are only a small number of individuals. But on the other side there are hundreds of thousands of workers, with their wives and children. Who is to defend their interests and care for them? The whole community of the people! Indeed, it is its duty to do so. Therefore the whole community cannot be made to bear the burden of economic disasters without according it the right of influencing and controlling economic life and thus avoiding catastrophes.

In the years 1932/33, when the German economic system seemed definitely ruined, I recognized even more clearly than ever before that the salvation of our people was not a financial problem. It was exclusively a problem of how industrial labour could best be employed on the one side and, on the other, how our agricultural resources could be utilized.

This is first and foremost a problem of organization. Phrases, such as the freedom of the economic system, for example, are no help. What we have to do is use all available means at hand to make production possible and open up fields of activity for our working energies. If this can be successfully done by the economic leaders themselves, that is to say by the industrialists, then we are content.

But if they fail, the folk-community, which in this case means the State, is obliged to step in for the purpose of seeing that the working energies of the nation are employed in such a way that what they produce will be of use to the nation, and the State will have to devise the necessary measures to assure this. In this respect the State may do everything; but one thing it cannot do - and this was the actual state of affairs we had to face - is to allow 12,000 million working hours to be lost year after year.

For the folk-community does not exist on the fictitious value of money but on the results of productive labor, which is what gives money its value.

This production, and not a bank or gold reserve, is the first cover for a currency. And if I increase production I increase the real income of my fellow-citizens. And if I reduce production I reduce that income, no matter what wages are paid out.

Members of the Reichstag: Within the past four years we have increased German production to an extraordinary degree in all branches. And the whole German nation benefits by this increase. For if there is a demand today for very many million tons of coal more than formerly, this is not for the purpose of superheating the houses of a few millionaires to a couple of thousand degrees, but rather because millions of our German countrymen are thus enabled to purchase more coal for themselves with their increased income.

By giving employment to millions of German workers who had hitherto been idle, the National Socialist Revolution has brought about such a gigantic increase in German production. That rise in our total national income guarantees the market value of the goods produced.

And only in such cases where we could not increase this production, owing to certain conditions that were beyond our control, there have been shortages from time to time; but these bear no proportion whatsoever to the general success of the National Socialist struggle.

The four-year plan is the most striking manifestation of the systematic way in which our economic life is being conducted. In particular this plan will provide permanent employment in the internal circulation of our economic life for those masses of German labour that are now being released from the armament industry.

One sign of the gigantic economic development which has taken place is that in many industries today it is quite difficult to find sufficient skilled workmen. I am thankful that this is so; because it will help to place the importance of the worker as a man and as a working force in its proper light; and also because in doing so - though there are other motives also - we have a chance of making the activities of the party and its unions better understood and thus securing stronger and more willing support.

Seeing that we insist on the national importance of the function which our economic system fulfils, it naturally follows that the former disunion between employer and employee can no longer exist. But the new State will not and does not wish to assume the role of entrepreneur. It will regulate the working strength of the nation only in so far as such regulation is necessary for the common good. And it will supervise conditions and methods of working only in so far as this is in the interests of all those engaged in work. Under no circumstances will the State attempt to bureaucratize economic life. The economic effects that follow from every real and practical initiative benefit the people as a whole. At the present moment an inventor or an economic organiser is of inestimable value to the folk community. For the future the first task of National Socialist education will be to make clear to all our fellow-citizens how their reciprocal worth must be appreciated. We must point out to the one side how there can be no substitute for the German worker and we must teach the German worker how indispensable are the inventor and the genuine business leader. It is quite clear that under the aegis of such an outlook on economic life, strikes and lock-outs can no longer be tolerated. The National Socialists State repudiates the right of economic coercion. Above all contracting parties stand the economic interests of the nation, which are the interests of the people.

The practical results of this economic policy of ours are already known to you. Throughout the whole nation there is a tremendous urge towards productive activity. Enormous works are arising everywhere for the expansion of industry and traffic. While in other countries strikes or lock-outs shatter the stability of national production, our millions of productive workers obey the highest of all laws that we have in this world, namely the law of common sense.

Within these four years which have passed we have succeeded in bringing about the economic redemption of our people; but we realise at the same time that the results of this economic work in town and city must be safeguarded. The first danger that threatens us here is in the sphere of cultural creativeness. And that danger comes from those who are themselves active in that sphere. For our fellow-countrymen who are engaged in artistic and cultural productivity today, or are acting as custodians and trustees of cultural works, have not the necessary intuitive faculties to value and appreciate the ideal products of human genius in this sphere.

The National Socialist Movement has laid down the directive lines along which the State must conduct the education of the people. This education does not begin at a certain year and end at another. The development of the human being makes it necessary to take the child from the control of that small cell of social life which is the family and entrust his further training to the community itself.

The National Socialist Revolution has clearly outlined the duties which this social education must fulfil and, above all, it has made this education independent of the question of age. In other words, the education of the individual can never end. Therefore it is the duty of the folk-community to see that this education and higher training must always be along lines that help the community to fulfil its own task, which is the maintenance of the race and nation. For that reason we must insist that all organs of education which may be useful for the instruction and training of the people have to fulfil their duty towards the community. Such organs or organisations are: Education of the Youth, Young Peoples Organisation, Hitler Youth, Labour Front, Party and Army - all these are institutions for the education and higher training of our people. The book press and the newspaper press, lectures and art, the theatre and the cinema, they are all organs of popular education.

What the National Socialist Revolution has accomplished in this sphere is astounding. Think only of the following:

The whole body of our German education, including the press, the theatre, the cinema and literature, is being controlled and shaped today by men and women of our own race. Some time ago one often heard it said that if Jewry were expelled from these institutions they would collapse or become deserted. And now what has happened? In all those branches cultural and artistic activities are flourishing. Our films are better than ever before and our theatrical productions today in our leading theatres stand supreme and alone in comparison with the rest of the world. Our press has become a powerful instrument to help our people in bringing their innate faculties to self-expression and assertion, and by so doing it strengthens the nation. German science is active and is producing results which will one day bear testimony to the creative and constructive will of this epoch.

It is very remarkable how the German people have become immune from those destructive tendencies under which another world is suffering. Many of our organisations which were not understood at all a few years ago are now accepted as a matter of course: the Young Folk, the Hitler Youth, BDM., Women's Association, Labour Service, SA, SS, NSKK, but above all the Labour Front in its magnificent departments - they are all building stones in that proud edifice which we call The Third Reich.

This consolidation of the internal life of our German nation also establishes a united front towards the outside world. I believe that it is here that the National Socialist Revival has produced the most marvellous results.

Four years ago, when I was entrusted with the Chancellorship and therewith the leadership of the nation, I took upon myself the bitter duty of restoring the honour of a nation which for fifteen years had been forced to live as a pariah among the other nations of the world. The internal order which we created among the German people offered the conditions necessary to reorganise the army and also made it possible for me to throw off those shackles which we felt to be the deepest disgrace ever branded on a people. Today I shall bring this whole matter to a close by making the following few declarations:

First: The restoration of Germany's equality of rights was an event that concerned Germany alone. It was not the occasion of taking anything from anybody or causing any suffering to anybody.

Second: I now state here that, in accordance with the restoration of equality of rights, I shall divest the German Railways and the Reichsbank of the forms under which they have hitherto functioned and shall place them absolutely under the sovereign control of the Government of the German Reich.

Third: I hereby declare that the section of the Versailles Treaty which deprived our nation of the rights that it shared on an equal footing with other nations and degraded it to the level of an inferior people found its natural liquidation in virtue of the restoration of equality of status.

Fourth: Above all, I solemnly withdraw the German signature from that declaration which was extracted under duress from a weak government, acting against its better judgement, namely the declaration that Germany was responsible for the war.

Members of the German Reichstag: The re-vindication of the honour of the German people, which was expressed outwardly in the restoration of universal military service, the creation of a new air force, the reconstruction of a German navy and the reoccupation of the Rhineland by our troops, was the boldest task that I ever had to face and the most difficult to accomplish.

Today I must humbly thank Providence, whose grace has enabled me, who was once an unknown soldier in the War, to bring to a successful issue the struggle for the restoration of our honour and rights as a nation.

I regret to say that it was not possible to carry through all the necessary measures by way of negotiation. But at the same time it must be remembered that the honour of a people cannot be bartered away; it can only be taken away. And if it cannot be bartered away it cannot be restored through barter; it must simply be taken back.

That I carried out the measures which were necessary for this purpose without consulting our former enemies in each case, and even without informing them, was due to my conviction that the way in which I chose to act would make it easier for the other side to accept our decisions, for they would have had to accept them in any case. I should like to add here that, now that all this has been accomplished, the so-called period of surprises has come to an end.

As a State which is now on an equal juridical footing with all the other States, Germany is more conscious than ever that she has a European task before here, which is to collaborate loyally in getting rid of those problems that are the cause of anxiety to ourselves and also to the other nations.

If I may state my views on those general questions that are of actual importance today, the most effective way of doing so will be to refer to the statements that were recently made by Mr. Eden in the British House of Commons. For those statements also imply the essentials of what must be said regarding Germany's relations with France. At this point I should like to express my sincere thanks for the opportunity which has been given me by the outspoken and noteworthy declarations made by the British Foreign Secretary.

I think I have read those statements carefully and have understood them correctly. Of course, I do not want to get lost among the details, and so I should like to single out the leading points in Mr. Eden's speech, so as to clarify or answer them from my side. In doing this, I shall first try to correct what seems to me to be a most regrettable error. This error lay in assuming that somehow or other Germany wishes to isolate herself and to allow the events which happen in the rest of the world to pass by without participating in them, or that she does not wish to take any account whatsoever of the general necessities of the time.

What are the grounds for the assumption that Germany wants to pursue a policy of isolation? If this conjecture of a German policy of isolation should be a conclusion drawn on the basis of assumed German intentions, then I would like to clarify here that I do not believe that any State could ever be deliberately disinterested in the events happening in the rest of the world, especially when this world is as small as the Europe of today. I believe that if a State truly needs to resort to such an attitude, then the most that can be said is that it has been forced to do so under the coercion of a foreign will imposed upon it. Now, in the first place, I should like to assure Mr. Eden that we Germans do not in the least want to be isolated and that we do not at all feel ourselves isolated.

During recent years Germany has entered into quite a number of political agreements with other States. She has resumed former agreements and improved them. And I may say that she has established close friendly relations with a number of States. Our relations with most of the European States are normal from our standpoint and we are on terms of close friendship with quite a number. Among all those diplomatic connections I would give a special place in the foreground to those excellent relations which we have with those States that were liberated from sufferings similar to those we had to endure and have consequently arrived at similar decisions.

Through a number of treaties which we have made, we have relieved many strained relations and thereby made a substantial contribution towards an improvement in European conditions. I need remind you only of our agreement with Poland, which has turned out advantageous for both countries, our agreement with Austria, and the excellent and close relations which we have established with Italy. Further, I may refer to our friendly relations with Hungary, Yugoslavia, Bulgaria, Greece, Portugal, Spain etc. Finally, I may mention our cordial relations with a whole series of nations outside of Europe.

The agreement which Germany has made with Japan for combatting the movement directed by the Comintern is a vital proof of how little the German Government thinks of isolating itself and how little we feel ourselves actually isolated. Furthermore, I have on several occasions declared that it is our wish and hope to arrive at good cordial relations with all our neighbours.

Germany has steadily given its assurance, and I solemnly repeat this assurance here, that between ourselves and France, for example, there are no grounds for quarrel that are humanly thinkable. Furthermore, the German Government has assured Belgium and Holland that it is ready to recognise and guarantee these States as neutral regions in perpetuity.

In view of the declarations which we have made in the past and in view of the existing state of affairs, I cannot quite clearly see why Germany should consider herself isolated or why we should pursue a policy of isolation. From the economic standpoint there are no grounds for asserting that Germany is withdrawing from international cooperation. The contrary is the truth. On looking over the speeches which several statesmen have made within the last few months, I find that they might easily give rise to the impression that the whole world is waiting to shower economic favours on Germany but that we, who are represented as obstinately clinging to a policy of isolation, do not wish to partake of those favours. To place this whole matter in its true light, I should like to call attention to the following bare facts:

1. For many years the German people have been trying to make better commercial treaties with their neighbours and thus to bring about a more active exchange of goods. And these efforts have not been in vain; for, as a matter of fact, German foreign trade has increased since 1932, both in volume and in value. This is the clearest refutation of the assertion that Germany is pursuing a policy of economic isolation.

2. I do not believe, however, that there can be a lasting economic collaboration among the nations on any other basis than that of a mutual exchange of commercial wares and industrial products. Credit manipulation may perhaps have a temporary effect, but in the long run economic international relations will be decisively influenced by the volume of mutual exchange of goods. And here the state of affairs at the present moment is not such that the outside world would be able to place huge orders with us or offer prospects of an increase in the exchange of goods even if we were to fulfil the most extraordinary conditions that they might lay down. Matters should not be made more complicated than they already are. If international commerce be sick, that is not due to Germany's refusal to assist it, but is due to the fact that disorder has invaded the industrial life of the various nations and has influenced their relations with one another. But Germany cannot be blamed for these two things, and especially not National Socialist Germany. When we assumed power the world economic crisis was worse than it is today.

I fear, however, that I must interpret Mr. Eden's words as meaning that in the carrying out of the four years plan he sees an element of refusal on Germany's side to participate in international collaboration. Therefore I wish it to be clearly understood that our decision to carry out this plan is unalterable. The reasons which led to that decision were inexorable. And since then I have not been able to discover anything whatsoever that might induce us to discontinue the four years plan.

I shall take only one practical example: In carrying out the four years plan our synthetic production of rubber and petrol will necessitate an annual increase in our consumption of coal by a margin of something between 20 and 30 million tons. This means that an extra quota of thousands of coal miners are assured of employment for the rest of their active lives. I must really take the liberty of asking this question: Supposing we abandon the German four years plan, then what statesman can guarantee me some economic equivalent or other, outside of the Reich, for these thirty million tons of coal? And that is the crux of the matter.

I want bread and work for my people. And certainly I do not wish to have it through the operation of credit guarantees, but through solid and permanent labour, the products of which I can either exchange for foreign goods or for domestic goods in our internal commercial circulation.

If by some manipulation or other Germany were to throw these 20 or 30 million tons of coal annually on the international market for the future, the result would be that the coal exports of other countries would have to decrease. I do not know if a British statesman, for example, could face such a contingency without realising how serious it would be for his own nation. And yet that is the state of affairs.

Germany has an enormous number of men who not only want to work but also to eat. And the standard of living among our people is high. I cannot build the future of the German nation on the assurances of a foreign statesman or on any international help, but only on the real basis of a steady production, for which I must find a market at home or abroad. Perhaps my scepticism in these matters leads me to differ from the British Foreign Secretary in regard to the optimistic tone of his statements. I mean here that if Europe does not awaken to the danger of the Bolshevic infection, then I fear that international commerce will not increase but decrease, despite all the good intentions of individual statesmen. For this commerce is based not only on the undisturbed and guaranteed stability of production in one individual nation but also on the production of all the nations together. One of the first things which is clear in this matter is that every Bolshevic disturbance must necessarily lead to a more or less permanent destruction of orderly production. Therefore my opinion about the future of Europe is, I am sorry to say, not so optimistic as Mr. Eden's. I am the responsible leader of the German people and must safeguard its interests in this world as well as I can. And therefore I am bound to judge things objectively as I see them.

I should not be acquitted before the bar of our history if I neglected something - no matter on what grounds - which is necessary to maintain the existence of this people. I am pleased, and we are all pleased, at every increase that takes place in our foreign trade. But in view of the obscure political situation I shall not neglect anything that is necessary to guarantee the existence of the German people, although other nations may become the victims of the Bolshevic infection. And I must also repudiate the suggestion that this view is the outcome of mere fancy. For the following is certainly true: The British Foreign Secretary opens up theoretical prospects of existence to us, whereas in reality what is happening is totally different. The revolutionizing of Spain, for instance, has driven out 15,000 Germans from that country and has seriously injured our trade. Should this revolutionizing of Spain spread to other European countries then these damages would not be lessened but increased.

I also am a responsible statesman and I must take such possibilities into account. Therefore it is my unalterable determination so to organize German labour that it will guarantee the maintenance of my people. Mr. Eden may rest assured that we shall utilize every possibility offered us of strengthening our economic relations with other nations, but also that we shall avail ourselves of every possibility to improve and enrich the circulation of our own internal trade.

I must ask also whether the grounds for assuming that Germany is pursuing a policy of isolation are to be found in the fact that we have left he League of Nations. If such be the grounds, then I would point out that the Geneva League has never been a real League of all Peoples. A number of great nations do not belong to it or have left it. And nobody has on this account asserted that they were following a policy of isolation.

THE CASE FOR GERMANY.

I think therefore that on this point Mr. Eden misunderstands our intentions and views. For nothing is farther from our wishes than to break off or weaken our political or economic relations with other nations. The contrary is the truth. **I have already tried to contribute towards bringing about a good understanding in Europe and I have often given, especially to the British people and their Government, assurance of how ardently we wish for a sincere and cordial cooperation with them.** I admit that on one point there is a wide difference between the views of the British Foreign Secretary and our views; and here it seems to me that this is a gap which cannot be filled up.

Mr. Eden declares that under no circumstances does the British Government wish to see Europe torn into two halves. Unfortunately, this desire for unity has not hitherto been declared or listened to. And now the desire is an illusion. For the fact is that the division into two halves, not only of Europe but also of the whole world, is an accomplished fact.

It is to be regretted that the British Government did not adopt its present attitude at an earlier date, that under all circumstances a division of Europe must be avoided; for then the Treaty of Versailles would not have been entered into. This Treaty brought in the first division of Europe, namely a division of the nations into victors on the one side and vanquished on the other, the latter nations being outlawed. Through this division of Europe nobody suffered more than the German people. That this division was wiped out, so far as concerns Germany, is essentially due to the National Socialist Revolution and this brings some credit to myself.

The second division has been brought about by the proclamation of the Bolshevic doctrine, an integral feature of which is that they do not confine it to one nation but try to impose it on all the nations.

Here it is not a question of a special form of national life in Russia but of the Bolshevic demand for a world revolution. If Mr. Eden does not look at Bolshevism as we look at it, that may have something to do with the position of Great Britain and also with some happenings that are unknown to us. But I believe that nobody will question the sincerity of our opinions on this matter, for they are not based merely on abstract theory. For Mr. Eden Bolshevism is perhaps a thing which has its seat in Moscow, but for us in Germany this Bolshevism is a pestilence against which we have had to struggle at the cost of much bloodshed. It is a pestilence which tried to turn our country into the same kind of desert as is now the case in Spain; for the habit of murdering hostages began here, in the form in which we now see it in Spain. National Socialism did not try to come to grips with Bolshevism in Russia, but the Jewish international Bolshevics in Moscow have tried to introduce their system into Germany and are still trying to do so. Against this attempt we have waged a bitter struggle, not only in defence of our own civilization but in defence of European civilization as a whole.

In January and February of the year 1933, when the last decisive struggle against this barbarism was being fought out in Germany, had Germany been defeated in that struggle and had the Bolshevic field of destruction and death extended over Central Europe, then perhaps a different opinion would have arisen on the banks of the Thames as to the nature of this terrible menace to humanity. For since it is said that England must be defended on the frontier of the Rhine she would then have found herself in close contact with that harmless democratic world of Moscow, whose innocence they are always trying to impress upon us. Here I should like to state the following once again:

The teaching of Bolshevism is that there must be a world revolution, which would mean world-destruction. If such a doctrine were accepted and given equal rights with other teachings in Europe, this would mean that Europe would be delivered over to it. If other nations want to be on good terms with this peril, that does not affect Germany's position. As far as Germany itself is concerned, let there be no doubts on the following points:

1. We look on Bolshevism as a world peril for which there must be no toleration.

2. We use every means in our power to keep this peril away from our people.

3. And we are trying to make the German people immune to this peril as far as possible.

It is in accordance with this attitude of ours that we should avoid close contact with the carriers of these poisonous bacilli. And that is also the reason why we do not want to have any closer relations with them beyond the necessary political and commercial relations; for if we went beyond these we might thereby run the risk of closing the eyes of our people to the danger itself.

I consider Bolshevism the most malignant poison that can be given to a people. And therefore I do not want my own people to come into contact with this teaching. As a citizen of this nation I myself shall not do what I should have to condemn my fellow-citizens for doing. I demand from every German workman that he shall not have any relations with these international mischief-makers, and he shall never see me clinking glasses or rubbing shoulders with them. Moreover, any further treaty connections with the present Bolshevic Russia would be completely worthless for us. It is out of the question to think that National Socialist Germany should ever be bound to protect Bolshevism or that we, on our side, should ever agree to accept the assistance of a Bolshevic State. For I fear that the moment any nation should agree to accept such assistance, it would thereby seal its own doom.

I must also say here that I do not accept the opinion which holds that in the moment of peril the League of Nations could come to the rescue of the member States and hold them up by the arms, as it were. No, I don't believe that. Mr. Eden stated in his last address that deeds and not speeches are what matters. On that point I should like to call attention to the fact that up to now the outstanding feature of the League of Nations has been talk rather than action.

There was one exception and in that case it would probably have been better to have been content with talk. In this one case, as might have been foreseen, action was fruitless.

Hence, just as I have been forced by economic circumstances to depend on our own resources principally for the maintenance of my people, so also I have been forced in the political sphere. And we ourselves are not to blame for that.

Three times I have made concrete offers for armament restriction or at least armament limitation. These offers were rejected. In this connection I may recall the fact that the greatest offer which I then made was that Germany and France together should reduce their standing armies to 300,000 men; that Germany, Great Britain and France, should bring down their air force to parity and that Germany and Great Britain should conclude a naval agreement. Only the last offer was accepted and it was the only contribution in the world to a real limitation of armaments.

The other German proposals were either flatly refused or were answered by the conclusion of those alliances which gave Central Europe to Soviet Russia as the field of play for its gigantic forces. Mr. Eden speaks of German armaments and expects a limitation of these armaments. We ourselves proposed this limitation long ago. But it had no effect because, instead of accepting our proposal, treaties were made whereby the greatest military power in the world was, according to the terms of the treaties and in fact, introduced into Central Europe. In speaking of armaments it would be well to mention in the first instance the armaments possessed by that Power which sets the standard for the armaments of all others.

Mr. Eden believes that in the future all States should possess only the armament which is necessary for their defence. I do not know whether and how far Mr. Eden has sounded Moscow on the question of carrying that excellent idea into effect, and I do not know what assurances they have given from that quarter. I think, however, that I ought to put forward one point in this connection. It is quite clear that the measure of a country's defensive armament should be in proportion to the dangers which threaten that country. Each nation has the right to judge this for itself, and it alone has the right. If therefore Great Britain today decides for herself on the extent of her armaments everybody in Germany will understand her action; for we can only think of London alone as being competent to decide on what is necessary for the protection of the British Empire. On the other hand I should like to insist that the estimate of our protective needs, and thus of the armament that is necessary for the defence of our people, is within our own competency and can be decided only in Berlin.

I believe that the general recognition of these principles will not render conditions more difficult but will help to release tension. Anyhow Germany is pleased at having found friends in Italy and Japan who hold the same views as ourselves and we should be still more pleased if these convictions were widespread in Europe. Therefore nobody welcomed more cordially than we did the manifest lessening of tension in the Mediterranean, brought about by the Anglo-Italian agreement. We believe that this will first of all lead to an understanding which may put a stop to, or at least limit, the catastrophe from which poor Spain is suffering. Germany has no interests in that country except the care of those commercial relations which Mr. Eden himself declares to be so important and useful. An attempt has been made to connect Germany's sympathy for Nationalist Spain with some sort of colonial claims. Germany makes no colonial claims against countries which have taken no colonies from her. Further, Germany herself has suffered so much under the tribulations of Bolshevism that she will not exploit the same tribulations in another nation in order to take something from another people in their time of weakness, or to extort something from them for the future. Our sympathies with General Franco and his Government are in the first place of a general nature and, secondly, they arise from a hope that the consolidation of a real National Spain may lead to a strengthening of economic possibilities in Europe. We are ready to do everything which in any way may contribute towards the restoration of order in Spain.

But I think that the following considerations should not be left out of account:

During the last hundred years a number of new nations have been created in Europe which formerly, because of their disunion and weakness, were of only small economic importance and of no political importance at all. Through the establishment of these new States new tensions have naturally arisen. True statesmanship, however, must face realities and not shirk them. The Italian nation and the new Italian State are realities. The German nation and the German Reich are likewise realities. And for my own fellow citizens I should like to state that the Polish nation and the Polish State have also become realities. Also in the Balkans nations have reawakened and have built their own States. The people who belong to those States want to live and they will live. The unreasonable division of the world into nations that have and nations that have not will not remove or solve that problem, no more than the internal social problems of the nations can be simply solved through more or less clever phrases.

For thousands of years the nations asserted their vital claims by the use of power. If in our time some other institution is to take the place of this power for the purpose of regulating relations between the peoples, then it must take account of natural vital claims and decide accordingly. If it is the task of the League of Nations only to guarantee the existing state of the world and to safeguard it for all time, then we might just as well entrust it with the task of regulating the ebb and flow of the tides or directing the Gulf Stream into a definite course for the future.

But the League of Nations will not be able to do the one or the other. The continuance of its existence will in the long run depend on the extent to which it realises that the necessary reforms which concern international relations must be carefully considered and put into practice.

THE CASE FOR GERMANY.

The German people once built up a colonial Empire without robbing anyone and without violating any treaty. And they did so without any war. That colonial Empire was taken away from us. And the grounds on which it was sought to excuse this act are not tenable.

First: It was said that the natives did not want to belong to Germany.
Who asked them if they wished to belong to some other Power? And when were these natives ever asked if they had been contented with the Power that formerly ruled them?

Second: It is stated that the colonies were not administered properly by the Germans.
Now, Germany had these colonies only for a few decades. Great sacrifices were made in building them up and they were in a process of development which would have led to quite different results than in 1914. But anyhow the colonies had been so developed by us that other people considered it worth while to engage in a sanguinary struggle for the purpose of taking them from us.

Third: It is said that they are of no real value.
If that is the case then they can be of no value to other States also. And so it is difficult to see why they deny them to us.

Moreover, Germany has never demanded colonies for military purposes, but exclusively for economic purposes. It is obvious that in times of general prosperity the value of certain territories may decrease, but it is just as evident that in times of distress such value increases. Today Germany lives in a time of difficult struggle for foodstuffs and raw materials. Sufficient imports are conceivable only if there be a continued and lasting increase in our exports. Therefore, as a matter of course, our demand for colonies for our densely populated country will be put forward again and again.

In concluding my remarks on this subject I should like to note a few points concerning the possible ways which may lead to a general pacification of Europe, which might also be extended outside Europe.

1. It is in the interests of all nations that the individual countries shall possess internally stable and orderly political and economic conditions. They are the most important conditions for lasting and solid economic and political relations between the peoples.

2. The vital interests of the different peoples must be frankly recognised. Mutual respect for these vital interests alone can lead to the appeasement of the essential needs of the nations.

3. The League of Nations, to be effective, must be reformed, and must become an organ of the evolutionary concept, and must not remain an organ of inactivity.

4. The relations of the people towards one another can only be regulated and solved on a basis of mutual respect and absolute equality.

5. It is impossible to make one nation or another responsible for armaments or for limitation of armaments, but it is necessary to see this problem as it really is.

6. It is impossible to maintain peace among the nations so long as an international irresponsible clique can continue their agitation unchecked.

A few weeks ago we saw how an organised band of international war mongers spread a mass of lies which almost succeeded in raising mistrust between two nations and might easily have led to worse consequences than actually followed.

I greatly regret that the British Foreign Secretary did not categorically state that there was not one word of truth in those calumnies about Morocco which had been spread by these international war mongers. Thanks to the loyalty of a foreign diplomat and his Government, it was possible to clear up this extraordinary situation immediately. Supposing another case arose in which it turned out impossible to establish the truth so readily, what then would happen?

7. It has been proved that European problems can be solved properly only within certain limits. Germany is hoping to have close and friendly relations with Italy. May we succeed in paving the way for such relations with other European countries. The German Reich will watch over its security and honour with its strong army. On the other hand, convinced that there can be no greater treasure for Europe than peace, it will always be a reasonable supporter of those European ideals of peace and will be always conscious of its responsibilities.

8. It will be profitable to European peace as a whole if mutual consideration be always shown for the justified feeling of national honour among those nationalities who are forced to live as a minority within other nations.

This would lead to a decisive lessening of tension between the nations who are forced to live side by side, and whose State frontiers are not identical with the ethnical frontiers.

In concluding these remarks I should like to deal with the document which the British Government addressed to the German Government on the occasion of the occupation of the Rhineland.

I should like first to state that we believe and are convinced that the British Government at that time did everything to avoid an increase of tension in the European crisis, and that the document in question owes its origin entirely to the desire to make a contribution towards disentangling the situation of those days.

Nevertheless, it was not possible for the German Government, for reasons which the Government of Great Britain will appreciate, to reply to those questions.

We preferred to settle some of those questions in the most natural way by the practical building up of our relations with our neighbours; and I should like to state that, complete German sovereignty and equality having now been restored, Germany will never sign a treaty which is in any way incompatible with her honour; with the honour of the nation and of the Government which represents it; or which otherwise is incompatible with Germany's vital interests and therefore in the long run cannot be kept.

I believe that this statement will be understood by all. Moreover, with all my heart I hope that the intelligence and goodwill of responsible European Governments will succeed, despite all opposition, in preserving peace for Europe. Peace is our dearest treasure.

Whatever contributions Germany can make towards preserving it, these she will make.

Before concluding my address today I should like to give a short sketch of the tasks that lie ahead of us.

In the carrying out of the Four Years Plan lies our first task. It will call for gigantic efforts but eventually it will turn out a great blessing for our people. Its purpose is to strengthen our national economic system in all its branches. The execution of it is guaranteed. All those great works which have been started apart from this plan will be continued. Their purpose is to promote the health of the nation and make life more pleasant. Building extensions will be systematically carried out in some of our large cities, as an externalization of the spirit that actuates this great epoch of the resurrection of our people. The foremost task will be the reconfiguration of Berlin into a real and true capital of the German Reich. Therefore, just as I have previously done for the construction of our roads, I have today appointed a General Building Inspector for Berlin, who shall be in charge of the architectural remodelling of the Reich's capital city and of bringing order to the chaos of Berlin's city planning to date. And that order will be based on such spacious plans as will be worthy of the National Socialist Movement and also of the German metropolis. We have allotted a period of twenty years for the carrying out of this plan.

May the Almighty God grant us a time of peace in which to bring this gigantic work to completion. Parallel therewith, the Capital of the Movement (Munich), the Party Metropolis (Nuremberg), and the Free City of Hamburg will be remodelled and extended on large lines.

But this work will only be the counterpart of a general cultural development which we wish to see taking place in Germany, as the crowning achievement to the restoration of our internal and external freedom.

And, finally, it will be one of our future tasks to give the German people a Constitution which will be in harmony with the real life of our people, as that life has developed politically. This Constitution will place its seal on this life for all time to come and will be an imperishable and fundamental law for all Germans.

As I look back on the great work that has been done during the past four years you will understand quite well that my first feeling is simply one of thankfulness to our Almighty God for having allowed me to bring this work to success. He has blessed our labours and has enabled our people to come through all the obstacles which encompassed them on their way.

I have had three extraordinary friends in my life. In my youth it was Poverty, which was my companion for many years. When the Great War came to a close it was the profound anguish that I felt over the downfall of our people. This anguish seized me and determined the path I had to follow. Since January 30th four years ago I have made the acquaintance of the third friend - anxiety for the people and the Reich, which have been entrusted to my guidance. From that time this anxiety has never left my side and will probably remain a faithful companion until the end of my days. But how could a man bear the burden of this anxiety were it not for the faith he has in his mission and which enables him to trust that He who is above us all sanctions my work. Destiny has often decreed that men who have a special mission to fulfil must be lonely and deserted. But here I wish to return thanks to Providence for having given me a group of faithful comrades who linked their lives with mine and have ever since fought at my side for the resurrection of our people. It is a great happiness for me that I did not have to walk among the German people as a man alone, but that at my side there was always a group of men whose names will endure in the history of Germany.

At this point I wish to thank my old fighting comrades who have stood by my side throughout all these years and who give me their help today either as Cabinet Ministers, Reichsstatthalter, Gauleiter, or in other positions under the Party or the State. During these days a tragedy is being enacted in Moscow which shows how highly we ought to value that loyalty which binds the leaders of a nation to one another. I further wish to express my sincere gratitude to all those who did not belong to the ranks of the Party but who in these recent years have been loyal assistants and comrades in governmental work and in other work for the nation. All of them belong to us, even though they may not wear the external insignia of our party community. I thank all those men and women who have assisted in building up our party organisations and working in them with success. But above all I have to thank the chiefs of our armed forces. They have enabled us to provide the National Socialist State with a National Socialist defence force, without placing any difficulties whatsoever in the way. Thus the Party and the defence forces are now the guarantors sworn to devote themselves to the preservation of our national existence.

But we know that all our efforts would have been in vain if we did not have the loyal cooperation of hundreds of thousands of political leaders, innumerable officials and countless soldiers and officers, who did their work under the inspiration of the ideal of our national resurgence. And above all we must acknowledge that our success could not have been attained if we were not backed up by the united front of the whole people.

On this historic occasion I must once again thank all those millions of unknown Germans, from every class and caste, profession and trade and from all the farmsteads, who have given their hearts, their lives and their sacrifices, for the new Reich. And all of us, gentlemen and members of the Reichstag, hereby join together in tendering our thanks to the women of Germany, to the millions of those German mothers who have given their children to the Third Reich. During these four years every mother who has presented a child to the nation has contributed by her pain and her joy to the happiness of the whole people. When I think of that healthy youth which belongs to our nation, then my faith in the future becomes a joyful certainty. And it is with a profound feeling that I realise the significance of the simple word which Ulrich von Hutten wrote when he picked up his pen for the last time -

Deutschland.

For more books on this subject and many other little-known aspects of German history, please visit us at VersandbuchhandelScriptorium.com
and our sister site wintersonnenwende.com !

Featured publications include:

- *Gebt mir vier Jahre Zeit! Dokumente zum ersten Vierjahresplan des Führers.* Alfred-Ingemar Berndt. Zentralverlag der NSDAP., Franz Eher Nachf. GmbH, München, ©1937. Reprint by The Scriptorium ©2002.

- *Hitlers Versuche zur Verständigung mit England.* Dr. jur. Heinrich Rogge. Junker und Dünnhaupt Verlag, Berlin, ©1940.

- *Was die Welt nicht wollte: Hitlers Friedensangebote 1933-1939.* Dr. Friedrich Stieve. Zentralverlag der NSDAP., Franz Eher Nachf. GmbH., Berlin ©1940,
as well as the English translation:
- *What the World Rejected: Hitler's Peace Offers 1933-1939.* Dr. Friedrich Stieve. Published under the auspices of the Deutsche Informationsstelle, ©1940.

More titles are being added regularly in German and English!

www.ingramcontent.com/pod-product-compliance
Lightning Source LLC
Chambersburg PA
CBHW072152100526